Preschool To Prison

Elvis Slaughter, M.S.C.J.

ISBN: 978-0-9965932-8-1

Published: Fall 2017

For information about bulk purchase, please contact:

Elvis Slaughter
P. O. Box 314
Calumet City, IL 60409

Eslaugh108@aol.com

Library of Congress Control Number: 2017914894

WWW.WORLDPRESSPUBLISHING.COM

Printed in the United States of America

PRESCHOOL TO PRISON

Elvis Slaughter, M.S.C.J.

Printed in the United States of America
www.worldpresspublishing.com

Contents

Summary

In this seminal work, *Preschool to Prison*, crime expert Elvis Slaughter takes aim at the genesis of crime in modern society. Having lived with career criminals during his experience at one of the largest prison systems in the nation, Slaughter raises a thought-provoking question: is the journey to prison determined by the school, environment, or parent?

For the answer, Slaughter illustrates the seven-year cycles of life and how each phase influences an individual's decision-making process. With examples from real-life situations, the crime expert shows how even the most gifted individuals could tread on a path of crime.

Writing in an engaging tone, Slaughter aspires to help develop responsive solutions for the society, where everyone, including parents, school administrators, and members of the community, collaborate to raise responsible children. As the saying goes, "It takes a village to raise a child," the implication is to create enabling elements that influence the decision-making process during the various stages of an individual's development.

"There can be no keener revelation of a society's soul than the way in which it treats its children."

— Nelson Mandela,
Former President of South Africa

Prologue

When it has to do with child upbringing, one question that easily comes to mind is this: can poor parenting actually turn a child into a delinquent? Well, the simple answer is yes. Several studies have demonstrated a variety of environmental and hereditary factors that show a causal relationship with juvenile delinquency. Based on research, it is believed that individual, community, and social conditions and the interactions of the child influence their behavior. Also, antisocial and delinquent behaviors are the result of a complex combination of both biological and genetic factors, as well as environmental factors, which start from the fetal development stage and continue throughout life (Bock & Goode, 2007). Although many children attain the age of adulthood without getting involved in serious delinquent behavior, despite multiple risks, it is quite difficult to identify the particular children who will engage in serious crime when they become adults. From childhood to teenage and then adulthood, humans undergo a series of development and changes that could be caused by biological, social, and environmental factors (Loeber et al., 2003). Are you wondering how to identify early indicators of criminal behavior and possibly stop the "cradle to prison pipeline?" This book serves as a guide to help parents, educators, and caregivers identify early signs of problem behavior in children, teenagers, and adults. Based on research, it has been confirmed that the best time to prevent an adult from engaging in criminal behavior is early, soon after a child is born. (Loeber et al., 2003). *Preschool to Prison* will help every individual understand the possible risk factors that could be indicators of teenagers or adults heading toward crime. It will enlighten parents, correctional institutions, law enforcement agencies, and caregivers of the behaviors that could lead children, teenagers, or adults to crime; why they engage in criminal behavior; and provide effective solutions to help them avoid criminal behavior. It will also educate teenagers and adults about the negative effects of getting involved in criminal behavior and how to avoid getting involved in crime. The cost of crime affects both parents, the community, and the government, and having the right information will help to greatly reduce the rate of crime in our society.

Introduction

As humans, we go through massive changes in life every day, and sometimes we get so busy, we don't really notice these changes. Understanding the changes we pass through will help us take full advantage of the development. The seven cycles of life start with the infant stage, which is the first cycle of human life, corresponding to the four years of life where we develop several characteristics faster than at other stages of life. During this stage, the infant is wholly dependent upon caregivers and parents for survival. The first four years from birth are the beginning of everything, and this period serves as the foundation upon which every other structure will be built. During the first three years of life, children change from complete physical dependence to independence, with several basic self-help and mobility skills. Although the precise timeline may differ from child to child, generally all newborns experience a gradual progression and development while transitioning from infants to young children. It's quite important for parents and caregivers to identify the rapid pace of growth and maturation of children from the time of birth to five years old. When assessing the risk of clinically significant child problem behavior, much emphasis is placed on parenting and other factors that might be able to compromise parental functioning, such as depression, teen parenthood, and social support. Other factors that may affect the developing brain, like prenatal drug use and prematurity, should also be considered.

The second life cycle is childhood, which covers the ages of 4 to 13 years. Within this period, we develop character and personal intelligence. Childhood is actually the building block on which adolescence and adulthood will be built. During this stage, the child is suscep-tible to learn habits and behaviors (Braverman, 2013). It's important to note a child's experience in the early years affects how the brain of the child works, their ability to form trusting relationships, and how they respond to stress. During this period, the child's brain undergoes tremendous growth, thereby setting the stage for social and emotional development. Also, during this period, children form basic motor abilities, start understanding their feelings and the feelings of others, and their thinking becomes more complex. Actually, the brain of a child doubles in size in the first year and reaches 80 percent of its adult volume by age three. The interactions of babies and adults help shape a baby's brain architecture, and this supports the devel-opment of communication and social skills. Whatever happens to the child in the first years of life is directly related to the child's long-term cognitive, emotional, and social outcomes all through his or her adulthood. The social and emotional development of a child is complex, and it actually involves different areas of growth. It includes attachment, which is the emotional bond between a parent, caregiver and the child; emotional regulation, which is the child's ability to control emotions and reactions to the environment; temperament, which has to do with the way a child acts and responds to caregivers, different situations, and strangers; and the child's social skills, which has to do with a child's ability to get along with other people.

Next is teenage and early adulthood, which is the third cycle of life. This stage covers ages 14 to 22 and is often linked with impulsive activity toward expression, lust, and love. During adolescence, puberty takes place, and gradually people begin to separate more from their parents and become independent. At this stage, juvenile delinquency sets in. According to research, there are two types of delinquents: those in whom the onset of severe antisocial behavior starts early; and childhood and delinquents, in whom this onset actually coincides with their entry into adolescence. Both cases provide communities, families, and systems the chance to intervene and help prevent the onset of antisocial behavior and the involvement of the justice system. Available information from research indicates that a more effective period to prevent the "cradle to prison pipeline" is as close as possible to the pipeline. Early intervention effectively prevents the onset of delinquent behavior and assists in the development of a youth's assets and resilience (Youth.gov).

The adult life cycle, the fourth cycle, starts at the age of 23. Many people are inclined to act more maturely during this stage, and they make decisions based more on logic than impulse.

The next cycle is the fifth stage, which is adulthood. Ptolemy believed it to be the matured adulthood stage. Sometimes at this stage, people feel their life has passed them by.

The age of 55 is the next cycle, which is the stage of retirement. This is a period when people develop a sense of wisdom and perspective.

The seventh cycle is the elderly stage and represents the last stage of life, which starts at the age of 67. This is the stage where people slow down on their desire for adventure, which continues until the end of existence (Meek, P).

Several theories have attempted to explain why people commit crime, and it is believed biological and social environment factors that will lead to criminal behavior are the two major reasons they do. Twenty first-century criminologists focused on a wide range of factors while trying to explain why people commit crimes. The factors included biological, psychological, social, and economic factors. In most cases, the combination of these factors provides the reason why people engage in crime. The early identification of risk factors and problem behaviors will go a long way in preventing the individual from committing crime (Andrews & Bonta 1998). Therefore, it is important that parents and caregivers learn effective prevention strategies from the early stage of life to ensure criminal behaviors identified in children are adequately nipped in the bud.

CHAPTER 1

Parental and Non-Parental Child Care (Newborn-2 Years)

THE EFFECTS OF CHILD MALTREATMENT ON CHILD DEVELOPMENT

The early maltreatment of a child can significantly alter the child's normal developmental arc and leave the victim with significant long-term impairments. It's also important that health care professionals who render care for maltreated children consider the consequences of the previous abuse for the child's adaptation and development when faced with a variety of long-term behavior issues, whether the children reside with foster families, birth families, or adoptive families. There is an increase in the number of documented evidence that shows the great relationship between adverse experiences in early childhood and a host of complications, both psychological and medical, that manifests throughout the childhood years and later in adult life (Stirling et al., 2008).

The Adverse Childhood Events Studies have illustrated that child neglect, abuse, and other circumstances that disrupt the parent-child relationship, are mainly associated with many leading causes of adult death, such as cancer, stroke, and heart disease and with heavy health service utilization. These disparate consequences, such as suicide, depression, diabetes, hypertension, alcohol, cigarette smoking, other substance abuse, and fractured bones, bear compelling evidence to the vulnerability of children to stressful experience (Felitti et al., 1998).

On a daily basis, pediatricians see children before, during, and after adverse events, including children who suffer the effects of trauma, which include physical and sexual abuse, separation and loss, parental neglect, and witnessing violence. In most cases, children with severe, chronic, or pervasive stress levels will experience difficulty in overcoming their persistent psychological and physiological responses to earlier stress. They may experience lingering symptoms of post-traumatic stress disorder, such as anxiety, sleeping difficulties, violent behavior, school failure, and oppositional behavior (Stirling et al., 2008).

Problematic behavior may continue long after the neglect or abuse have ceased, despite the consistent and attentive parenting by adoptive, birth, or foster parents who have successfully changed their own behaviors. Unless healthcare professionals identify the relationships of the frequent behavior problems to their remote antecedents, their interventions will most likely be inefficient, and at worst ineffective or counterproductive. It's important to note that the primary health care professional holds the first and perhaps most critical link for children and caregivers: to enable them to understand that the child's unsatisfactory response to stress may have actually been a biologically based adaptation to the child's abnormal world, and the consequence is persisting problem behaviors (Stirling et al., 2008).

THE SOCIAL DEVELOPMENT PHASE OF A CHILD (0-2 YEARS)

The social development of a child greatly determines how the child will relate with other children and further in life while interacting with other people. Babies are born social creatures, and when parents learn how to help a child's social skills, the child will flourish. From the earliest days, babies begin to connect and obtain information from their caregivers. Newborns are capable of imitating facial expression, which demonstrates an understanding of how the actions of others relate to their own. Within weeks, babies start cooing and smiling intentionally and respond to their caregiver's communications (Anthony, M).

From age 0-2 years, children are often engaged in relationships, trying to develop a deep sense of being nurtured and loved. During this stage of their life, they seek a relationship that engenders security, trust, and a sense of optimism. If they succeed, then they would have mastered the basic psychosocial goals of this stage and will advance in their development with a strong and secure sense of the world, as well as their place within it. It's important to note that it's only from a place of secure attachment that babies are secure enough to explore the larger world around them (Anthony, M).

9-12 Months

Babies become interested in exploration between the age of 9-12 months, and this drive actually coincides with their learning to crawl and walk. This stage usually leads to new adventures away from the nurturing caregivers, and at this point they start to point to objects, which is a significant developmental milestone that helps illustrate the baby's ability to establish a shared focus with another. Pointing, therefore, allows their interaction to expand and include actions and objects, enlarging the babies' ability to help them learn through more complex interactions (Anthony, M).

09-18 Months

Between 9-18 months, babies also develop a more sophisticated understanding of themselves and other people. Around 18 months, a baby can recognize that the image in the mirror is actually himself, rather than just a different toddler. Within this period, children start having stranger anxiety, where babies often hang back from less well-known adults. At this stage, they also show displeasure when parents or primary caregivers leave them or put them in the care of another person. According to a British psychologist, John Bowlby, the attachment serves a very useful function, because it allows a kind of equilibrium between the baby's increasing need to explore and the baby's need for a secure base to help protect and guide the baby. A child can carry the sense of protection and security a caregiver provides when exploring, thereby allowing the baby to continue to meet the extra developmental drive for exploration and discovery (Anthony, M).

Two Years

This stage is regarded as the stage of autonomy vs. shame and doubt. At this stage, it's quite easy to see the full appearance of the child's will and the parents' patience, and the parents' ability to successfully respond to a child's needs will significantly affect the outcome of this stage. Children at this stage develop their first interest and an increased desire for autonomy. With the encouragement of parents or caregivers, children can explore and expand on these drives and interests. They usually develop self-sufficient behavior, such as learning how to dress and feed themselves, and a sense of autonomy. It's important to note that with punitive responses, punishment or demands beyond the child's capabilities, they often retreat into shame and doubt (Anthony, M).

Common Effects of Poor Parental Care on the Development of the Child

The consistent love and care of a parent help shape the developmental journey of a child, and parents who know how to embrace the role of parenting with much enthusiasm will help the child acquire skills that maximize life potential. Poor parental care negatively impacts the rapid growth and change that often occurs in the developing child from infancy to adolescence, with long-term consequences. Take a look at some areas where infants may experience poor parental care (Swain, B).

MALNUTRITION

In early childhood, physical growth and development usually occur at an amazing pace, and poor nutrition presents a risk for the impaired physical development of the child. According to Child Welfare Information, children who don't get sufficient iron in their daily diet, for instance, may exhibit difficulties in reaching cognitive and motor milestones; and they experience anxiety, depression, and problems developing social skills. When parents fail to provide adequate nutrition, it results in stunted growth and less efficient transmission of neural signals in the brain (Swain, B).

INSECURE ATTACHMENT

One of the issues that children encounter in their early development is insecure attachment. A child's attachment is the ongoing relationship that exists between the child and parent, and a developing child who forms a secure attachment feels safe and acknowledges his needs will be met and will be supported with the challenging tasks of learning to self-regulate his emotions. Also, a secure attachment serves as a security blanket that releases the child to direct attention to other equally challenging tasks of investigating the environment and learning new skills. According to the American Academy of Pediatrics, parents who are unpredictable, unavailable, or inattentive jeopardize the development of a secure attachment by not allowing their child to feel protected (Swain, B).

REACHING MILESTONES

Children or infants need stimulation from parents in the form of hugs, praise, and motivation to achieve developmental milestones. Parental apathy usually exists when parents don't invest time in their child's developmental progress. According to Child Welfare Information Gateway, neglected children exhibit delays in physical, language, cognitive, and social development. Children build a positive self-concept and validate a secure attachment to parents when the dad or mom cheers their efforts to balance on one foot, share a toy, and complete potty training (Swain, B).

Brain Development

Short-lived episodes of stress are not often detrimental to the growth of a child, and they actually may help the child learn how to adapt and respond to stressors in the future. However, parents serve as barriers between their children and the more harmful types of stress, and when parents don't shield their child from chronic, erratic, or harsh forms of stress, these stressors will modify the developing child's brain. According to the children's development website Zerotothree. org, the results of this damage include long-term challenges related to academic success, as well as physical, behavioral and psychological problems. When a child consistently lives in a dangerous environment, the brain of the child focuses more on survival and less on abstract thought (Swain, B).

The Impact of Nonparental Care on Early Childhood

Over the past few decades, there has been a constant increase in the number of children (preschool-aged children) who spend a significant amount of time in non-parental care, and concerns about the impact of non-parental care on child development exist. Currently, about two-thirds of young children frequently attend some form of childcare, and an average child spends 32 hours weekly in these settings (Laughlin, 2010). Also, the transition of infants into non-parental care usually occurs rapidly after childbirth.

Based on a NICHD Study of Early Child Care (1997a), the typical child enters child care at about three months. Within the first year of life, 80 percent of children experience regular participation in non-parental arrangements, while more than one-third have a minimum of three distinct caregivers. The most common form of childcare setting for preschool-aged children is relative care, which accounts for 41 percent. This is followed by a center (23 percent), and family-based arrangements (13 percent) (Laughlin, 2010). Depending on the quality and duration of non-parental care, it can actually improve cognitive outcomes and protect children from disadvantaged homes or possibly pose risks to children (McCartney, 2004).

There is evidence indicating Early Childhood Education and Care (ECEC) in the first three years for children benefit children's social, cognitive, and language development in both the long-term and short-term. *However, low-quality childcare can lead to a dual risk for children, especially from low-income families, leading to possible deficits in cognitive and language development.* Also, there is evidence to suggest high levels of childcare, especially group care in the first two years, may elevate the risk for developing antisocial behavior; however, based on subsequent research, there are indications it may be related to high levels of poor quality of child care, particularly in centers in the first year. The main concern is not really non-parental care but the quality of early childhood education and care.

The low level of early child education and care is a major concern, and some have actually argued that in the United States, for instance, government-funded preschool programs, such as Head Start, child care centers, and state-funded prekindergarten, provide services that are of mediocre quality—or worse—and children who attend such average centers may gain little cognitive boosts. They argue that greater benefit could be obtained by improving the quality of these programs (Haskins et al., 2011). Others are of the view that publicly funded preschool in the U.S. actually narrows the achievement gap between the non-poor and poor groups by as little as five percent, due to the prevalence of low-quality programs, and that the gap could be narrowed by up to 50 percent if the quality were improved (Pianta et al., 2009). There is evidence to suggest that a starting age from two years onward is most effective for preschool education.

QUALITIES OF A GOOD PRESCHOOL AND CHILDCARE FACILITY

Based on research, the following quality characteristics of early year provision are important for enhancing a child's development:

- A well-trained staff that is committed to their work with children

- Adult-child interaction that's not only responsive and affectionate but also available

- A developmentally appropriate curriculum that has educational content

- Facilities that are safe, clean, and accessible to parents

- Proper staff development that ensures stability, continuity, and improving quality

- Ratio and group sizes that enable staff to interact properly with children

- Supervision that maintains consistency

To enhance stronger outcomes, early child education and care should be characterized by structural features of quality and ongoing supports to teachers, so as to ensure that the children's experiences (those provided through activities and interactions) are rich in content and stimulation, while also being emotionally supportive (Melhuish et al., 2014).

The Impact of Trauma on Child Development

"It is easier to build strong children than to repair broken men."

— Frederick Douglass, abolitionist and statesman

The negative effects of trauma in child development are a major reason for the poor outcome of the lives of preschoolers. What is child maltreatment? It refers to a child who is physically, emotionally, or sexually abused or neglected, exploited, or even exposed to domestic violence by a parent or caregiver. These kinds of maltreatment can lead to childhood trauma, which can be defined as either simple or complex. *A simple trauma is a single isolated and definable traumatic event.* A single case of maltreatment can even be traumatic and lead to a wide range of potentially negative short-term psychological and behavioral responses from the affected child. Such behavioral responses include:

- Dissociation

- Fear

- Loss of trust

- Inability to regulate emotions

- Attachment disorders and several others

There are several studies that confirm that children who suffer maltreatment are more likely than other children to be arrested and/or referred for delinquent offenses.(English, 1998; Fagan, 2005; Jonson-Reid et al., 2000; Kelley, et al., 1997; Widom, 1996; Widom et al., 2001; Zingraff et al., 1993).

Also, children who have experienced maltreatment are more likely to commit offenses when they become adults (English et al., 2002; Fagan, 2005; Mersky et al., 2010).

Based on a study by the National Institute of Justice (NIJ), maltreated children were actually 11 times more likely than a matched control group to be arrested by law enforcement agents and 2.7 times more likely to be arrested when they become adults (English et al., 2004). Children who were abused and/or neglected are more likely to become delinquent at a younger age, and they're more likely to commit a violent offense (Lemmon, 1999; Ryan et al., 2007; English, 1998; English et al., 2002; Kelley et al., 1997; Widom, 1996; Widom & Maxfield, 2001).

The more violence children are exposed to, the higher the possibility that they will become delinquent. For instance, maltreated children who also witnessed domestic violence were more likely to become delinquent than children who were exposed to only one example of such violence (Chiodo et al., 2008). Also, it's important to note that children who were chronically maltreated stand a higher risk of being more delinquent than other children who experienced only one or two incidents of maltreatment (Ryan & Testa, 2005; Stewart et al., 2008).

CONCLUSION

The possibility of children in childcare to develop and maintain a good relationship with parents greatly depends upon the parents' ability to provide sensitive care at home (NICHD Early Child Care Research Network, 1997). It's important that parents establish a balance between home and childcare settings and continue to provide a variety of intimate interaction that's not available in childcare centers (Ahnert et al., 2003; NICHD, 1999). It's been discovered that long hours in childcare and stressful parent-child relationships are associated with anger and aggression in preschool children, whereas healthy relationships between children and caregivers help reduce behavior problems and aggression (Belsky et al., 2007; NICHD, 2003). The transition from home to childcare centers can be stressful for many children, so care providers should help the children manage their responses to this stress (Ahnert et al., 2004).

Considering the fact that children can greatly benefit from experiences in non-parental childcare, childcare has to be of a good quality and should also render access to a variety of positive social relationships (Lamb, 2000). In order to ensure child care environments are developmentally appropriate, the adult-child ratio must be kept low. Also, the group size and composition should be considered as mediators of the quality of individual care provider-child relationships (NICHD, 2007).

It's important that informed parents and regulations ensure and demand the highest possible quality of child care, because caring for other people's children in groups needs different care strategies than caring for ones' own child. Care providers should be valued by the society, enriched by serious and careful education and training, and well-compensated.

Research has suggested there is a link between the quality of parent-child attachment and the outcomes much later in life, like the levels of self-esteem, social skill, and aggressive behavior. Preschool children who have parents who are uninvolved, harsh, or rejecting are more likely to exhibit overactive, aggressive, noncompliant, and impulsive behavior (Campbell, 1995, P.113). A secure bond with parents enables the child to develop a positive self-image and helps the child learn to trust the parents, which may also transfer to a general perception of other people being reliable and safe too. Parents create a secure base when they're responsive, available, and a reliable source of safety and comfort to the child, and this serves as a good foundation for general interpersonal skills. The way children interact with parents is important, and the temperament of the child might actually influence the way parents treat the child, which makes the bond dyadic in nature (Teacher Law, November 2013).

CHAPTER 2

The Effects of Trauma in Child Development

One of the great paradoxes of our lives as humans is that we're constantly passing through massive and enormous changes daily. The early years of childhood are actually the beginning of everything, and it's also the foundation upon which the later structures will be built. Even at birth, babies already have the given potential of creativity, intelligence, and personality. However, this potential has to come to terms with its environment, and this includes the body. Human beings cannot have awareness without consciousness, and there won't be thinking without the right tools of thought, such as ideas, language, and concepts. During the early years, we're moved greatly by the instincts of the need for love, hunger, protection, and support, along with pain and the impact of the environment in which we find ourselves. During this period, we build up the inner mental structures that will enable us to think, feel, and be aware of ourselves as individuals in the future (Crisp, T).

Actually, during the first seven years, something mysterious happens in our lives. During this cycle, we pass through an incredible process of learning. This learning process includes motor movements, relationships with ourselves and our environment, and speech. That means learning about the responses we get from others and developing habits of response, which may be difficult to change later in life. During this period, we're completely dependent on loved ones for our needs, whether emotional, social, or physical. Children feel great jealousy and anger or pain when loved ones relate to anyone else, threaten to leave, or are lost (Crisp, T).

AGE AND DEVELOPMENTAL STAGE (2-4 YEARS)

When dealing with a child, it's imperative that we consider the developmental age of the child. Parents and caregivers no doubt want children to reach their full potential while keeping an eye on their development and providing the necessary support that will help them meet their milestone. It's important to note that all children and young people vary in their individual development, and the impact of trauma and abuse can have a major effect on the typical development pathways. The following points should guide every caregiver and parent while guiding a child through their developmental stage:

- The development of a child does not occur evenly or in a straight line.

- The achievement of specific developmental milestones depends greatly on the opportunities the child has to practice them, and on the experience available to them.

- The pace of development of a child occurs more rapidly in the early years than any other time in life.

- Development delays in an area will actually impact the development in others.

- The general health of a child affects development and behavior. Minor illnesses will no doubt have short to medium-term effects, while chronic ill-health can have long-term effects. Also, nutritional deficiencies negatively impact the developmental progression of a child (Department of Human Services, 2007). Parents and caregivers with concerns about the child's progress should seek medical advice.

STAGE DEVELOPMENT TASK (2-4 YEARS)

1. Developing a conscience

2. Uses up to 50 (or more) words and communicates in simple sentences

3. Develops impulse control

4. Helps with simple household chores

5. Asserts preferences

6. Participates in imitation/fantasy play

7. Small motor coordination (e.g. holds crayons with fingers, not fists)

8. Large motor development

9. Develops a sense of time

10. Walks well, runs, stops, steps up, and squats

11. Answers simple "what" and "what do" questions

12. Uses the spoon and cup all independently

13. Jumps, throws, climbs using great balance

14. Names 5 to 6 body parts on themselves

15. Asks a lot of "why" and "what" questions

16. Uses 2 to 3-word sentences regularly (Daniel et al., 2010).

TIPS FOR PROMOTING HEALTHY CHILD DEVELOPMENT

As parents and caregivers, it's important to enhance the development of the child in any positive way. The following tips will help in promoting healthy development:

- Ask your child to pick up toys and put them away after playing. This will help the child develop motor skills.

- In the event the child is under foot while preparing dinner, you can ask the child to carry light non-spill containers to the table for you.

- You can engage the child by running around a tree and back or through a maze of objects. This will provide the child with rigorous exercise and helps the child master turns and balance.

- Walking along a line on the ground will also help promote balance and concentration.

- Hopping on one foot, then the other, and skipping helps promote balance and strengthens the leg muscles.

- Read with the child, search for books with pictures and active stories, and then ask your child questions about the pictures, story, and characters.

- You can take the child on a fun, educational outing, such as the aquarium, zoo, or the children's museum, and encourage the child to ask questions regarding what he or she sees (ParentHelp123).

The Effects of Traumatic Stress on Children

"Each day of our lives, we make deposits in the memory banks of our children."

— *Charles R. Swindoll, Evangelical Christian pastor*

Sometimes, children who survived severe traumatic events, such as automobile accidents, house fires, natural disasters, or major medical illness, often complain of disordered sleep, altered emotional response to everyday situations, and intrusive "flashback" memories. Severe reactions of this nature and many more are particularly common after incidents of interpersonal violence, such as child abuse, terrorism, and domestic violence. In cases involving child abuse, neglect, or exposure to violence where the stresses are usually prolonged and unavoidable, it's been observed that long-term stress reactions are common and can often be devastating.

It has also been observed in patients suffering from the aftereffects of major early stress in their childhood, the offending stimulus—which is minor—sometimes seems to echo the previous abuse and produce an equivalent dramatic emotional reaction that is usually inappropriate to the provocation. Stimuli that often produce such reactions are regarded as *traumatic reminders* and may actually take many forms. *It's interesting to note that reaction to an old trauma may actually be triggered by a sound, smell, or other sensory input, and it may also be triggered by an action, date, or place.* During this kind of reaction, the brain engages in what seems to be an exaggerated form of pattern recognition, which is a common form of learning in which similar patterns of stimuli call forth a similar neuroendocrine (and therefore, behavioral) response (Bremner et al., 2003; Elzinga et al., 2003)._

Types of Symptoms

Symptoms can actually be classified into three main behavioral clusters:

- Re-experiencing through intrusive thoughts, "flashback" recollections, and dreams.

- Physiological hyperarousal in the form of hypervigilance and exaggerated startle response, sleep disturbance, and attention and concentration problems.

- Avoidance of reminders and numbing of responsiveness, which includes restricted range of effect, constriction of play, and social withdrawal.

A situation where disordered stress response persists long after the trauma is known as Post Traumatic Stress Disorder (PTSD) (Cook, 2003; American Psychiatric Association). It's unclear why some children develop PTSD after trauma, while others do not. Although the severity and chronicity of the initiating stress seem to be involved, other host factors, like social support and genetic variation, are also involved (Holbrook et al., 2005).

The diagnostic criteria for PTSD are actually the same in children as in adults, and they can be summarized as:

- An exposure to a traumatic event that involved the serious threat of death, which is accompanied by intense fear and terror.

- Numbing of general responsiveness and the avoidance of stimuli that triggered the re-experience (which is often seen in restricted range of effect, social withdrawal, and constriction play).

- The tendency to persistently re-experience the traumatic event, usually through intrusive thoughts, "flashback" recollections, and dreams.

- Persistent symptoms of arousal, which includes exaggerated startle, hypervigilance, and other physiological measures.

- The duration of the symptoms mentioned above for over one month, resulting in clinically significant distress or possibly impaired functioning (American Psychiatric Association, 2000).

These characteristics may manifest in developmentally different ways in children, such as extreme emotional liability or traumatic display with hair trigger-explosive responses to minor provocations (Eth, 2001; Pfefferbaum, 1997; Pynoos, 1993).

Research has revealed that anatomical changes correlate with a history of PTSD symptoms, which include smaller brain volumes and size differences in limbic structures. Caregivers of children with extremely difficult behaviors need to understand the fault is not entirely theirs and the child's. Such children are dealing with a physiological response that's unfamiliar to them, and they're also learning new and effective ways of responding themselves. Despite the fact that love and consistency are essential, they are usually not sufficient (De Bellis M.D et al., 1999; Teicher et al., 1999; Teicher et al., 2004).

THE EFFECTS OF EARLY STRESS

There is no doubt the seeds of adult dysfunction are sown in early childhood stress. There have been several instances, such as the lifelong effects of early malnutrition or exposure to toxins like lead or alcohol. However, it's remarkable that many of the dysfunctional behaviors have their origin not in some random organic dysfunction, but rather in the otherwise healthy brain's physiological adaptations to the abnormal world in which the developing children find themselves. Although these adaptations are initially useful, they have not prepared the child for existence in a larger or normal world outside the home.

The behaviors that may have been useful, even life-saving, in a neglectful or violent home, such as extreme passivity or hypervigilance will become the problem behaviors that are identified in school or in a child care, which are often interpreted as "attention deficit" or "daydreaming." Once such behaviors are established and internalized, the child's typical response to stimuli (the child's definition of normal) can actually be very difficult to change (Stirling et al., 2008).

There has been remarkable progress in the understanding of neuro-development in the past two decades. Once regarded as an enigmatic "black box," the brain is now viewed as a complex of specialized, inter-active organs constantly developing through interaction with each other and the environment. *It's interesting to note that this development is more dramatic in the first three years of life, as the young brain actually undergoes sweeping structural change as it not only senses but also adapts to the environment in which it finds itself.*

Neurons develop myelin sheaths and proliferate, developing myriad connections with others, all through the cranium. Some are strengthened with experience, developing more connections with other neurons. Also, others are cut back through a process known as apoptosis, which is the "pruning" of unused connections. Significant apoptosis is actually seen as early as four years of age, and this continues until the typical adult brain has lost almost half of the neuronal connections it possessed at the age of three. Presently, it's now understood that pruning is experience-dependent (its use strengthens neural pathways, while idleness marks others for demolition) (Stirling et al., 2008).

Conflicts in Brain Development of a Child

Unfortunately for the child, a brain specifically adapted to just one type of extreme environment is seldom optimized to perform in another, and this in itself would not really be an insurmountable problem. However, children raised in a violent, abusive, and neglectful home are usually denied the right tools to enable them to adapt to new and different surroundings. As earlier stated, abused children usually suffer impairments in their cognitive skills and language abilities. According to a recent study, 36 percent of preschoolers in foster care were found to be developmentally delayed, and no difference was found between the developmental effects associated with reported physical abuse, neglect, or sexual abuse (Rossman, 2001).

Such deficiencies may actually reflect prenatal insults or even postnatal contributors like malnutrition or toxic exposures, but they certainly correlate with inadequate parental care, especially during sensitive periods in early brain development, providing the child with less exposure to language and fewer opportunities necessary for cognitive development (Zimmer et al., 2006). Did you know one of the most important tasks of early childhood is learning to discriminate states of affect? That's quite true (Beeghley et al., 1996). Lacking good models, neglected or abused children may actually grow up unable to explain (or even understand) the difference between feelings such as sadness and anger. In extreme cases, this is known as alexithymia (the inability to "read" emotion), and without this very important perception, the ability to perceive the intention of others, or even monitor one's response, is lost and social learning is severely impaired. The human brain is most easily altered or adapted early in its life. Although there are thought to be few true "critical periods" after which alterations become impossible, early childhood may be thought of as a "sensitive period" for several forms of cognitive and most emotional learning. After this period, it becomes difficult to successfully establish new patterns of thinking or reacting (Institute of Medicine, 2000; Siegel, 1999). Consequently, an abused or neglected child is often asked to adapt to a new and different world but given inadequate neural and behavioral tools needed to do so.

Conclusion

The child's hypervigilance and inability to regulate emotional states after maltreatment may actually lead to challenging behaviors in interaction with others. In most cases, victims of previous abuse or neglect are far more often recognized as "problem children" than their peers, and they show a higher rate of diagnosis with attention problems and violent and oppositional behaviors. Most times, caregivers and teachers usually respond to these behaviors in the traditional fashion, becoming more brusque (and louder) and disciplining more strictly (often more punitive). Despite the fact that such responses from adults often result in normal children, they become problematic when the listener is hyper vigilant for threats and has difficulty controlling his or her own emotions. To a child physiologically adapted to a high-threat environment, a minor slight or even stern admonition can sound like the prelude to real danger, and when the child's exaggerated emotional response evokes an even stronger response, the child may mistakenly assume his or her initial reaction was warranted. Such responses inadvertently confirm the child's mistaken impression that indeed the world, in general, is a high-threat environment. This in effect is actually a positive feedback, because it reinforces the preceding behavior, the behavior that has negative consequences for the child and all those around the child. With reinforcement, neural adaptation (learning) actually continues. Although maltreated children's threat-adapted neuroanatomy can be perceived to determine their behavior, that behavior (through the responses of those around them) would be expected, in turn, to determine the further growth of their anatomy (Wodarski et al., 1990).

Across this continuum of outcome possibilities, present caregivers (whether birth parents, adoptive parents, or foster parents) are going to face challenges in appropriately responding to the child's physical and mental health needs. Birth parents who were initially neglectful and have stopped using drugs or abandoned a violent domestic situation, may now be consistent and attentive to their children, but they may find such children unresponsive to their best efforts. It's important to note that as abused children grow and develop, earlier trauma is revisited and reconsidered. Usually, a child who has learned to live with these abnormal responses will no doubt experience added challenges in dealing with them as an adolescent. Physiological changes and the onset of formal operational thought can actually complicate adjustment issues, and it's possible for problematic behavior to resurface in new and often dangerous forms. At this point, caregivers should be well prepared to help children respond constructively. Therapy should be provided and directed toward reshaping the child's perceptions and emotional responses while also helping the caregivers address their own behaviors. The failure to do so can lead to serious long-term consequences that may range from violent behavior to dangerous risk-taking to impaired domestic relationships (Styron et al., 1997; Alexander, 1993).

CHAPTER 3

Child Discipline and Its Effects on the Child

The major goal of parenting is not only to teach a child, but also assist the child in acquiring character traits such as integrity, competence, self-control, respectfulness, and honesty. These important traits do not come naturally to the infant or preschooler, but through the disciplinary process, children will acquire them to some degree. So what is discipline? It's the training of a child that is expected to produce specific character or pattern of behavior, especially the training that produces moral or mental improvement in the child (The American Heritage Dictionary, 2000).

Actually, in the context of parenting, the child discipline process comprises three primary components: instruction, encouragement, and correction. These three components are parental efforts that act upon the child's temperament within a milieu that's influenced by parental and environmental factors. The complex process yields a child outcome through a combination of several elements (mainly within the parents' control, especially at younger ages) (American College of Pediatricians, 2007).

Discipline is used mainly by parents to teach children about expectations, guidelines, and principles. They need to be regularly disciplined, taught right from wrong, and maintained safely. Usually, child discipline involves punishments and rewards to teach self-control, decrease undesirable behaviors, and increase desirable behaviors. It's very important to note that while the purpose of child discipline is developing and entrenching social habits in children, its ultimate goal is to foster sound morals and judgment so the children can develop and maintain self-discipline throughout the rest of their lives (Sarah S, 2012). It's actually summarized by this Bible verse: *"Train up a child in the way he should go, And when he is old he will not depart from it" (Proverbs 22:6 NKJV).*

Considering the fact that the beliefs, values, education, cultures, and customs of people vary widely along with age and temperament of the children, methods of discipline also vary widely. Presently, child discipline is a topic that attracts the attention of interested parties, such as the professional practice of behavior analysis, parenting, social work, developmental psychology, and several religious perspectives (Wikipedia).

The Discipline Process

As earlier mentioned, the discipline process comprises three components:

- **Instruction** - This happens to be the first and fundamental component of discipline. It's important that the expectations of a parent be clearly communicated and repetitively so as to begin to achieve compliance. As soon as the desired behavior is communicated, the consequence of the misbehavior must be made known to the child. Although the toddler may not understand the consequence of misbehavior as a result of preoperant cognition, with repetition, the child's behavior will be modified by the reinforcer and punisher responses. Older children will no doubt understand, and a volitional decision to defy or comply will be made consciously. Also, instructions can be nonverbally communicated to the children through parental modeling of proper behavior. It's important to note that poor behavior outcomes are usually associated with unclear or absent instructions and inconsistent parental expectations.

- **Encouragement** - This represents the reinforcer response in the behavioral model, and relative to the level of development of the child, it will take the form of physical affection, verbal praise, or material reward. Parents that use little encouragement and rely mainly upon harsh and excessive correction often fail to achieve optimal behavioral control.

- **Correction** - The punisher response in the behavioral model is correction, and it's often necessary when in spite of the encouragements, the child fails to adhere to instruction. This will involve redirection for the infant or distraction. At this stage, a brief expression of disapproval that could be verbal or nonverbal will help modify the child's behavior. As the assertiveness and mobility of a child mature, correction may actually require aversive punishers, such as physical discomfort or physical restraint. For an older preschooler, privilege removal and reasoning will gradually start being effective. Natural and logical consequences can also be effective modifiers of behavior, and they may preclude the need for additional corrective actions by parents with timely occurrence (Baumrind, 1973).

FACTORS THAT AFFECT THE DISCIPLINARY PROCESS

Several factors may affect the disciplinary process of a child, and it's important for parents to understand these factors and how they also influence the disciplinary process of their children.

PARENTAL FACTORS

Some parental factors, such as communication, nurturance, effective disciplinary skills, and stability of marriage, play a significant role in child discipline. Parents act as role models for acceptable and expected behavior (Behrman et al., 2002). Adult models greatly influence aggressive behavior in children, and parental consistency and predictability are very important in enhancing acceptable behavior in children. Delayed imposition of consequences, changing consequences, and irregular application of consequences are some practices that characterize parents of "out-of-control" children (Patterson, 1982).

Reactive versus proactive correction leads to very different outcomes, and a parent who actually takes the time to instruct and forewarn a child is more likely to get the desired behavior than a parent who impulsively corrects a child's uninstructed behavior. Another factor that is foundational to the disciplinary process is the parent-child relationship. It's important to note that children respond well if discipline occurs in the context of a warm and affectionate relationship and parental involvement in monitoring of the activities of a child positively affects child compliance (Bauman et al., 1998).

The result of negative parenting was properly summarized by Bauman and Friedman this way: "Ineffective parenting practices actually predict conduct disorder in childhood, which is also strongly associated with peer rejection, academic failure, and later involvement in chronic deviant behavior, which includes aggression. Also, family variables are consistent covariates for early forms of deviant behavior. **Families of antisocial children are often characterized by little positive parental involvement with the child, harsh, inconsistent discipline and poor monitoring and supervision.** Inept parenting practices, which also include non-contingent positive and negative reinforcers, mean coercive child behaviors are unwittingly reinforced" (Bauman et al., 1998).

Finally, another factor fundamental to the health of a society and the optimal development of a child is the father-mother married unit (Schneider et al., 2005). No doubt, marital harmony models respect for one another and provide a stable environment for emotional growth. Children raised in families with high levels of marital conflict are more likely to develop behavioral problems than those in families with low levels of conflict. **The instability of a marriage relationship can cause a child to reject the parent's values and defy their directives** (Cummings et al., 2002).

CHILD FACTORS

Several factors, such as the child's age, individual characteristics, and developmental level need to be considered when implementing child discipline. Innate temperament will obviously influence a child's tendency toward compliance, just like his energy level and individual attentiveness will, too. The birth order of a child can be a determinant; firstborn children are usually more compliant than their subsequent siblings. The age of a child influences the child's need for behavioral correction, with punishment frequently required and used during the preschool years (Dietz, 2000). These child factors generally influence which disciplinary measure parents should use in correcting their children and how it's implemented.

ENVIRONMENTAL FACTORS

Socioeconomic conditions, ethnicity, neighborhood composition, religiosity, and cultural views are some environmental factors that influence the effect of disciplinary measures on the child. Families with few socioeconomic resources usually perceive physical punishment as more favorable than non-physical punishment and achieve better behavioral control using it (Deater-Deckard et al., 1996). When the environmental risks are high, parenting practices that are firmer and more in control result in lower levels of young adolescent antisocial behavior (Eamon, 2002). Also, in neighborhoods where there is a prevalence of corporal punishment, its use doesn't lead to greater child behavioral problems (Simons et al., 2002).

THE LONG-TERM EFFECTS OF NOT DISCIPLINING A CHILD

Most times, parents are always eager to give kids everything they desire just to make them happy; however, parents that give too much often tend to spoil their children, and this can be very harmful to them developmentally and socially. There are several effects of spoiling a child:

- **Dependency** - Children who are spoiled by their parents can become overly dependent on their parents, and this can cause them to have difficulties in making themselves happy as adults. According to a research conducted on college-aged young adults, it was discovered that adults who were spoiled as children have a tendency to believe that being alone makes a person unhappy and that other people are the source of their happiness, rather than themselves.

- **Disrespect and Defiance** - This is a major characteristic of spoiled children, who are most likely to beg, whine, ignore, or even manipulate to get their way. Usually, spoiled children are so overindulged they don't even have to express themselves in any other way than through their negative behaviors. Rebellion can become a natural response in spoiled children who are overprotected and overindulged.

- **Highly Irresponsible** - When children are spoiled by their parents, they don't usually have to learn responsible behaviors. Spoiled children are unable to understand the concept of boundaries as adults, and this can develop into serious problems, such as gambling, drinking, spending, and overeating. Often, these children are not motivated and can be described as angry or lazy. As a result of lack of emotional maturity and having poor problem-solving skills, these adults that were spoiled as children might flounder and become unhappy with their lives.

- **Poor People Skills** - This could also be referred to as "poor relationship skills." Because while they were growing up, they didn't learn that relationships involve both give and take, spoiled children not only can have trouble making friendships but also keeping meaningful friendships. Spoiled children can be insensitive to other people's needs; they are prone to temper tantrums and have trouble deferring gratification. Considering the fact that other children might avoid children with such traits, spoiled children might become unhappy loners who don't even appreciate being by themselves (Scottsdale, 2015).

What Do Children Really Want?

Based on a large national study, it was discovered that what children really want from their parents is for them to:

- Understand their moods.

- Use constructive discipline.

- Make them feel loved and important.

- Be involved with their learning and schooling.

- Let them know what to expect (routines).

- Accept them just for who they are.

- Be present for important life events, such as performances, ball games, and teacher meetings (DeBord, K).

Parenting Tips for Children

It's much easier to give your child lots of affection and love; after all, you definitely love your child. However, disciplining a child is never an easy task. If parents really want their children to know right from wrong and grow up with good manners and self-esteem, then parents need to learn how to discipline their children properly, no matter how hard it may be. The following useful tips will help every parent discipline their children appropriately.

Be a Good Disciplinarian

Being a good disciplinarian means parents should understand the things that need to be done and the things that should not be done when handling their children. Some points to note include:

- **Consistency** - As a parent, if you truly want your children to be well-disciplined, then it's important to be consistent with your rules as expectations. The moment children discover that parents are liable to overlook their bad behaviors when parents are distracted, tired, or feel sorry for them, they may not likely know how to act properly every time. Being consistent with your expectations as a parent can be difficult sometimes, especially after working all day; however, it is something that needs to be done. Take note of the following points when ensuring consistency about your expectations:

o The moment you work out a good system of discipline for a child, keep it consistent. Once the child breaks or behaves badly, follow such actions with the same discipline consistently and avoid feeling sorry on a particular day.

o **It's also important that both parents of a child be involved in presenting a punishment for wrongdoing. Parents must present a united front and should avoid having a bad cop/good cop parent. That may cause the child to favor one parent over the other and lead to a strain in the relationship between the child and the parent involved.**

o **Maintain consistency, even in public.** Although this is easier said than done, because it can be embarrassing to experience a public tantrum, it's much better than giving children the impression that they can always get what they want if only they just throw a tantrum in public.

- **Children Need Boundaries** - When there are no boundaries, there will be no guidelines, and life without guidelines leads to insecurity. The parents happen to be a child's major source of security, and when parents' behavior shows they are not in control, this leads to uncertainties. Children push the limits because they need to be aware that limits are there and there is someone in charge, keeping them safe.

- **Respect Your Child**- Always bear in mind that the child is also a human being, no matter the age of the child and how frustrated a parent may be. If parents want children to respect authority, then it's also important that parents appreciate the fact that children are imperfect human beings with their wants and needs, and they actually need love and respect from their parents. As a parent, you will find the tips below useful in making sure you respect your child at all times:

o Avoid calling your child bad names or names that will lower the self-worth of your child or possibly make him or her feel worse. Choose better ways to say how you feel about the behavior of the child, rather than saying something like "You are so stupid."

o In a situation where you are very angry with the child as a result of his or her behavior, avoid saying anything until you calm down. This happens mostly when a child spoils something that's very expensive or precious and you are tempted immediately to start punishing the child. You may shout or even say words you will later regret. It's better to cool off before saying or doing anything.

o Parents should behave the way they want their children to behave by being a good role model. When this is not done, parents may be sending mixed signals with their own bad behavior.

o Always avoid situations where you act inappropriately and then apologize later for the bad behavior. In case you did, then apologize to the child and explain to the child that you shouldn't have acted that way. The child will apologize, too.

• **Show Empathy** - There is a big difference between being sympathetic and being empathetic. Empathy means being able to appreciate other people's feelings. When it comes to children, it's important that parents appreciate the children's problems, struggles, and feelings. Sympathy has to do with feeling sorry for the children when they are upset during bad behavior and making efforts to help them recover from the problem. Take note of the following tips when making efforts to empathize with your child:

- o It's important you understand the reasons your child behaved badly. Getting to know the reason will help you understand the pain or loss they feel and give you a better idea of how to help the child better.

- o Try and talk to your child about his or her feeling. Always acknowledge how your child feels while explaining to your child that his or her action is inappropriate.

- **Parents Should Communicate Their Expectation** - It's critical that parents let their children know exactly what they consider as good and bad behavior, as well as the consequences of exhibiting bad behavior. As soon as a child is old enough to understand the parents' needs, then parents should make it clear there will be consequences if a child does any bad thing. The tips below will help parents communicate their expectations to their children:

  - o Take time to talk to the child regarding good and bad behavior. As long as the child is old enough, the child should feel included in understanding what he or she did or did not do well and how to act next time.

  - o Before trying a new discipline technique, parents should first explain it to the child, even before the bad behavior happens. If this is not done, the child will be confused.

  - o Depending on the age of the child, a child can actually choose the rewards for good behavior if they are appropriate (wikiHow).

PARENTING AND ITS OUTCOME FOR CHILDREN

The methods that parents adopt in shaping their children's development have been long-standing sources of theorizing by philosophers, scientists, and other parents. Based on the outcome of a wide range of studies, the quality of the parent-child relationship is greatly associated with:

- Social competence - Lack of conflict, parental warmth, control, and monitoring appear to play a vital role in developing children's social skills.

- The quality of parent – The child relationship appears to be influential up until adulthood for social and behavioral outcomes (though there have been few long-term studies).

- In most cases, there is considerable stability in the quality of family relationship over time, especially when a secure bond of attachment between the children and parents exists.

- Genetic factors have an important influence on the individual differences in parent-child relationships. The links that exist between the quality of parent-child relationship and children's psychology adjustment are mediated partly by genetic influences.

- Aggressive 'externalizing' behavior and delinquency - **The more extreme the parents' circumstances, the worse the outcomes for the children, and the likelihood of psychological disturbance.**

- High-risk health behaviors, such as illicit drug use, alcohol use, smoking, sexually risky behavior, and in some studies, obesity can negatively impact parent-child relationships (Utting, 2007).

CONCLUSION

There are several methods of child discipline, and corporal punishment is no longer a popular method of punishing a child. New methods have been adopted by parents in most civilized nations of the world. The praise and rewards method, for instance, is one of the most commonly used methods that parents apply. Giving children spontaneous expressions of acknowledgment or appreciation when they behave well will serve as reinforcement for good behavior, and focusing on the bad versus good behavior will encourage good behavior in any given situation. Past behavior that's reinforced with praise is most likely to repeat in either the same or similar situation (Skinner, 1938).

Children can also be disciplined to behave well through natural consequences. It involves children learning from their mistakes. The duty of parents is to teach their children which behaviors are wrong. To do this, parents usually allow their children to make mistakes and let them have a firsthand experience of the natural results of their behavior. If a child, for instance, forgets to take his lunch to school, the child will no doubt be hungry and will not want such a mistake to occur again (Lareau, 2011). The choice of a method is what every parent needs to make and must have the best interest of the child as the key determinant of the method chosen.

CHAPTER 4

The Effects of Instability on Child Development

The early experiences of children no doubt affect their learning, health, and who they generally turn out to be in the future. Every child needs stable housing that's safe and adequate food that is nutritious. They need access to secure relationships, nurturing parents that are responsive, good medical care and standard learning opportunities both at school, in childcare settings, and at home. Based on available data from research, there is strong evidence to suggest a large number of children experience instability in their lives.

While parents strive to provide for their families financially, the severe stress they encounter may actually make it difficult for them to provide the much-needed care and attention their children need. Most children who grew up during periods of recession have experienced so much instability in their lives, and the absence of continuity and security in homes can have a strong, lasting impact on the emotional, physical, and cognitive development of the children. Instability has always been a longstanding issue most families experience; however, during difficult periods such as recession, it's always increased. Considering the advances in the study of toxic stress and the adverse effects it has on child development, there is an increasing need for us to understand what instability actually means for children and ways the negative effects can be prevented (National Scientific Council on the Developing Child 2007).

What Is Instability?

Although in social science, the word instability connotes change or discontinuity in an individual's experience, the operational definitions of instability vary based on field and are determined based on measures and data available for research. However, for the purpose of the topic being discussed, *"Instability is the experience of change in an individual's or family's circumstances where such change is involuntary, abrupt and/or towards a negative direction, and such change has every possibility of having adverse effects on the development of the child."* When changes occur, they don't occur in isolation. A disruption in a domain such as a parent's change of job or loss of job may actually lead to a disruption in another area, such as childcare, usually in a "domino effect" manner. Also, it's important to note the casualty of instability is not just one-dimensional; rather, it's a result of a series of complicated events that compound over time. The domino effect of instability is likely to be more visible among lower middle class and low-income families that lack assets and savings they can rely on during temporary periods of their transition (McKernan et al., 2009; Mills et al., 2010).

Parents may not be able to properly support their children in adapting to change when they lack control over change. The issue of instability has been examined and studied from various perspectives with the underlying belief that some kind of change and changes that take place at certain points in the lives of children actually predict negative outcomes for children (Moore et al., 2000).

Why Instability?

Children perform well in a stable and nurturing environment with a routine and a general understanding of what to expect from their daily lives. It's true that some changes are normal and anticipated for children; however, unexpected and dramatic disruptions in children's lives can be very stressful, and this will definitely affect the children's feeling of security. *"Within the context of supportive relationships with adults acting as a buffer against possible negative effects of instability, children are able to learn how to cope with adversity, regulate their emotions and adapt to their surroundings"* (National Scientific Council on the Developing Child, 2007). However, stress that's not buffered can escalate to extreme levels, which can be detrimental to a child's mental health and cognitive functioning (Evans et al., 2011; Shonkoff et al., 2011).

Based on a recent research from the National Scientific Council on the Developing Child, the experience of some level of stress is normal and essential for the healthy development of the child (National Scientific Council on the Developing Child 2007). Every day, young children encounter emotionally stressful events. For instance, on the first day at a childcare center, an infant will be separated from his or her mother and experience some form of stress. Such daily events actually produce positive stress, and this kind of stress is characterized by mild elevations in the levels of stress hormones and increase in heart rate.

The human body is empowered to respond to environmental stress in a way that will protect us from harm, and even experts view more moderate levels of stress as tolerable for children when buffered by supportive adults. However, children who are exposed to constant and strong adversity for a prolonged time are at risk of cognitive impairment and stress-related disease (National Scientific Council on the Developing Child, 2007).

The effect of toxic stress on a child is serious. It causes an overreaction of the stress response system, which causes the body to be in a constant heightened state of arousal. This state disrupts normal brain and organ development, and as a result it damages the brain architecture and neurocognitive systems. So, what's the implication of this damage? It leads to poor academic performance, lack of the ability to regulate emotions, and lack of social competence. Evidence suggests that adult cognitive abilities can be partly impaired by elevated chronic stress during childhood (Evans et al., 2009). Several domains of instability can affect the proper development of a child. Let's take a look at some types of instability.

ECONOMIC INSTABILITY

This could also be regarded as economic insecurity, and it has to do with a reduction in family income. Sometimes, families may or may not recover from a financial crisis. Family income may come from public income support, such as temporary cash assistance and earnings from a job (Mills et al., 2010). Based on research, two in five adults having children lose a quarter of their finance or income at least once at some point within a year, indicating that fluctuations in homes are actually common (Acs et al., 2009). Take a look at a summary of the major findings about the impact of economic stability on children:

- The child's cognitive development in early childhood is actually most sensitive to the experience of low income in the family.

- The experience of economic instability leads to increased material hardship, especially in situations where families lack personal assets.

- Although there are bodies of literature on economic instability and the relationship that exists between poverty and child development, there is limited literature on the effects of economic instability on the development of children.

- Low levels of income in a family negatively affect a child's social-emotional, academic, and cognitive outcomes, even after controlling for parental characteristics (Sandstrom et al., 2013).

Families without liquid assets that will serve as a backup experience greater material hardship than those with adequate savings. It's important to note that involuntary job loss and divorce account for the major cause of economic instability in homes, and many families find it difficult to recover from the instability. Based on available information from research, having a low family income during childhood strongly predicts more poor cognitive outcomes than low-income during adolescence or middle childhood (Sandstrom et al., 2013).

EMPLOYMENT INSTABILITY

The employment of parents greatly affects the economic security of families. The moment parents lose their jobs, their family is likely to suffer material hardship with fewer resources to assist in their child development (McKernan et al., 2009). Other factors that could also affect the economic situation of the family include the status of the unemployed parent (whether sole earner or not), the availability of a family savings, the length of the unemployment, and the availability of social safety net or assets, which can also influence the family's economic security (Isaac, 2013; McKernan et al., 2009). Although researchers have questioned how family spending, the outcomes of children, and economic security could be affected by employment instability, available information from research indicates that children with parents who have lost their jobs are at an increased risk of negative academic outcomes (Kalil et al., 2011; Kalil & Ziol-Guest, 2008; Stevens et al., 2011).

There is evidence to suggest that the loss of a job by a father may actually be more strongly related to a child's academic outcome than the loss of a mother's job. When it comes to dual-earner homes where the mother earns more than the father, the father's involuntary job loss is linked with a higher chance of grade repetition and school suspension or expulsion for school-aged children when compared to the loss of a job by a mother (Kalil et al., 2008).

Consequently, it was concluded by researchers that the negative effect of the loss of a job by a father may relate more to changes in family dynamics and stress that exist at home, and perhaps less with material hardship as a result of the loss of income. It's also been observed that the experience of a job loss, followed by long-term parental unemployment, actually predicts lower educational attainment for children. Children with middle-income parents who are unemployed for a period of six months or more at any point in their childhood have a lower chance of obtaining any postsecondary education by age 21, compared to their peers who have consistently employed parents (Kalil et al., 2011).

One of the main effects of the economic constraints that occur due to an unstable employment is that it makes it more difficult for parents to support their children's developmental needs, because families with a reduction in their income are likely to cut back on their spending, change their residence, and even end up in separation or divorce (Yeung et al., 1998). Also, a reduction in the level of income in the home can actually affect children in other ways. Family routines and schedules may not be predictable, and there will be a strain in parental relationship because parents will always focus on securing a new job (Kalil et al., 2011).

Take a look at a summary of the effects of employment instability on children:

- The effect of employment instability on grade retention is strongest for children who have parents with a high school education or less. Also, its effect on educational attainment is stronger in males and first-born children, and even stronger for blacks than whites.

- There is a link between parental employment instability and negative academic outcomes like lower educational attainment, grade retention, and internalizing and externalizing behaviors.

- Involuntary job instability results in worse child behavioral outcomes than when parents are engaged in full-time low-wage jobs, have fluctuating work hours, or voluntarily change their jobs.

- A father's job loss in a dual-income household may be more strongly associated with the children's academic outcomes than the loss of job by a mother, even when the father earns less than the mother (Sandstrom et al., 2013).

HOME INSTABILITY

Another major insecurity that affects children is family instability. The family structure and support greatly serves an important function in children's experiences. Based on the U.S. Census data of 2012, a total of 68 percent of children below the age of 18 years live in a two-parent home, while 28 percent live in single-parent homes, and most of the single parent households are headed by mothers (Census 2012, Table C2). Generally, the structures of families are diverse, even with adopted parents, married and unmarried parents, two-parent households, and cohabiting partners. Based on a recent survey, it's estimated that over one-third of children experience a change in family structure: a separation, the beginning or end of a cohabiting union, and (re)marriage, and all these take place between their birth and the end of 4th grade (Cavanagh et al., 2008).

The high rate of instability in families and increase in the number of children born outside marriage implies that about one-half of children will most likely temporarily live in single-parent homes. Although there have been several debates regarding the effects of new marriage or divorce on children (whether it's the underlying traits and behaviors of the parents or change of parental union that has the greatest impact on children), there are studies to indicate that parental divorce possesses the potential to cause short-term and long-term family crises (Amato, 2000). What family instability means for a child is either the loss of contact with a parent or the change of home environments as a result of financial constraint, the absence of social support and an increase in parental stress, leading to depression and general reduction in the quality of parenting. This does not suggest that there are no positive effects of changes in family structure on the child, provided such changes will strengthen the family's support system and reduce conflicts among parents (Craigie et al., 2012).

Take a look at a summary of the effects of family instability on children:

- Children are known to display more negative behaviors when they are deprived of material and emotional support needed at home to be able to handle family transition.

- Instability in homes is linked to academic difficulties and problem behaviors, and this occurs even at early ages.

- Family transitions that take place early in a child's development (before the age of six) and in adolescence seem to possess the strongest effects. Just as children are constantly in need of caregivers to help them develop secure attachment, adolescents also require role models, good parental support, and continuity of schools and residence to succeed.

- The problem behaviors in children are greatly increased when there are multiple changes in family structure (Sandstrom et al., 2013).

RESIDENTIAL INSTABILITY

Generally, there is a high mobility rate among homes in the United States. Did you know that in 2012, a total of 36.5 million people (a year and older), which is 12 percent of the U.S. population, changed their residences within the previous year? (U.S. Census Bureau, 2012) Despite the fact that moves are common in the United States, the effect of frequent or abrupt movement from one residence to another can be extremely stressful for children, because they need to detach themselves from what is familiar and adapt to new environments. Children not only pick up on negative cues but also on parental stress, and this can greatly weaken the children's level of security and increase their level of stress. When their stress level is increased, it could be detrimental to their development. The residential moves can also be extremely confusing and stressful for children who lack reasoning and language skills that will enable them to fully understand the situation they are facing and be able to communicate their thoughts and feelings (Rumbold et al., 2012). Available information from research highlights the importance of routines and organization within the children's home environment, and when it's not in place, children are definitely going to experience environmental confusion and chaos in the home (Matheny Jr. et al., 1995).

Based on research, it's evident that parents play a major role in shaping the children's experiences, and this role has a great impact on the effects of instability on children. On one hand, a stimulating and nurturing environment actually helps enhance a child's potential achievement; on the other hand, environmental deprivations and stressors inhibit the normal development of a child and can even lead to negative outcomes. The healthy development of children requires the enrichment and protection of children by adult caregivers. Parents are in the best position to provide their children with the external stimulation and support they need to develop, and they greatly determine the children's ability to cope and adjust when faced with stressful experiences (Shonkoff, 2013).

CONCLUSION

Presently, the healthy development of children is hindered by a dual set of obstacles. Many parents are struggling to feed and care for their families, as they live in unstable housing, work unstable jobs, deal with erratic childcare arrangements, and have unpredictable relationships. The sudden changes in homes usually lead to inconsistencies both within the home and outside the home. Also, there is insufficient funding for public programs that can support families and children in times of need (Sandstrom et al., 2013).

Despite the fact that, primarily, it's the duty of parents to ensure the well-being and healthy development of their children, there are also several government programs that play major roles in ensuring the healthy development and well-being of children, especially for children in low-income homes. These safety-net programs render financial assistance to homes in the form of subsidized housing, cash payments, food, or childcare. These forms of assistance help to alleviate the immediate effects of instability on children and their families. However, such programs can actually do more to ensure that children are stabilized by carefully considering if any administrative practices indirectly lead to instability. Additional efforts could be made to ensure skill-building and sound mental health of parents considering the central role they play in the effect of instability on children. The use of well-designed two-generational intervention programs focused on reducing parental and childhood stress, positive parenting, and strengthening family coping strategies can greatly help ease the effect of instability on children (Sandstrom et al., 2013).

CHAPTER 5

Early Warning Signs of Criminal Tendencies in Children: Aged 4-7 Years

CONDUCT DISORDER AND ANTISOCIAL BEHAVIOR IN CHILDREN

Globally, the most common mental health disorders of childhood and adolescence are conduct disorders, and they are also the most frequent reason for the referral to child and adolescent mental health services in Western countries. A great proportion of children and even young people who have conduct disorders actually grow up to become antisocial adults with impoverished and destructive lifestyles. There is an increase in the case of conduct disorders in childhood in Western countries, which is placing great personal and economic burden on people and society. This involves not just the social care agencies and health care services, but also other sectors of the society, such as the schools, family, the criminal justice agencies, and the police. So what is conduct disorder? It's an overarching term used in psychiatric classification, which refers to a persistent pattern of antisocial behavior where an individual breaks social rules persistently and engages in aggressive acts that upset other people (American Psychiatric Association, 2000).

Children between the ages of 4-5 are kindergarten students and at this age, the children are introduced to numbers, alphabets, the body, colors and communities. Other activities that they engage in includes, art making projects, listening to stories, learning about animals, plants and other science topics and participating in skits and dramatic productions. Ideally, the kindergarten offers the children a foundation for the crucial development of motivation, cognition, social skills and self-confidence (The National Academies Press, 2015).

APA (1993) discovered in a crucial study on youth, violence and antisocial-aggressive behavior that children and youth are increasingly becoming involved in violent behaviors, even at younger ages, and based on the report, poor parenting, academic achievement, and school factors are major influences that cause it. **It's important to note that the early appearance of behavioral problems in a child's preschool career happens to be the best predictor of adult incarceration, delinquency in adolescence, and gang membership** (Dishion, French, & Patterson, 1995; Reid, 1993). It has also been observed that children who grow into adolescence with challenging behaviors have the tendency to abuse alcohol and drugs, drop out of school, have greatly marginalized adult lives, be arrested, and die young (Lipsey & Derzon, 1998; Walker, Colvin, & Ramsey, 1995).

Several facts were listed in a research carried out by Walker et al., (1995) regarding adolescent delinquency. They stated that early antisocial behavior in children is a predictor of adolescent delinquency, and antisocial behavior can easily be identified in children at the early age of three or four. It was also observed that antisocial behavior that persists beyond the age of third grade has actually become chronic. The only hope children with antisocial behavior have is early intervention. **The researcher also disclosed that certain antisocial behavior patterns and high levels of aggression exhibited in kindergarten and preschool are not just correlated, but are greatly predictive of violent, criminal behavior in middle school, delinquent, and later adolescence and adulthood** (Zaroban, 2006).

DEFINITION OF ANTISOCIAL BEHAVIOR

What exactly is antisocial behavior? It has to do with disruptive acts characterized by overt and covert hostility and intentional aggression toward other people. It involves a repeated violation of social rules, a defiance of the rights of other people and authority, deceitfulness, reckless disregard for others and self, and theft. It can actually be identified in children as young as three or four years old, and if it's not checked, the behaviors will persist and possibly escalate over time and become a chronic behavioral disorder (Connor, 2002).

FACTS ABOUT ANTISOCIAL BEHAVIOR

Did you know between 4 and 6 million children in America have been identified with antisocial behavior problems? It is among the most common forms of psychopathology and accounts for half of all childhood mental health referrals. The gender difference in antisocial behavior patterns can be identified as early as age three or four. Presently, there has been less research into the nature and development pattern of antisocial behavior in girls. Pre-adolescent boys have a higher tendency to engage in overtly aggressive antisocial behavior than girls. While antisocial behavior in girls is indirect and relational, involving harmful social manipulation of others, boys exhibit more verbal and physical aggression. It might interest you to know that about half of all elementary school children who demonstrate antisocial behavior patterns actually continue to demonstrate these behaviors into adolescence, and as many as 75 percent of the adolescents who exhibit antisocial behaviors continue into early adulthood (Gale Encyclopedia of Children's Health, 2017).

The most antisocial five percent of children who are aged seven years are actually 500% to 1000% more likely to show indices of serious life failure at 25 years, such as criminality, leaving school without qualifications, drug dependency, unwanted teenage pregnancy, unemployment, etc. (Fergusson et al., 2005). Finally, it is important to note that about 90% of severe recurrent adolescent offenders displayed marked antisocial behavior in early childhood (Piquero et al., 2010).

Who Is Responsible for Children's Antisocial Behavior?

So, what is the source of the antisocial behavior children display? The factors that contribute to the antisocial behavior of a child varies; however, those factors will definitely include some form of family problems, which could include the following:

- Harsh or inconsistent disciplinary practices

- Marital discord

- Child abuse

- Learning or cognitive disabilities

- Health issues

- A frequent change in primary caregiver

Also, it has been observed that attention deficit/hyperactivity disorder is greatly associated with antisocial behavior. Parents need to understand that a child can exhibit antisocial behavior in response to a particular stressor, like divorce or the death of a parent, for a limited period of time. Children with antisocial behavior score high on traits of impulsiveness. However, they score low on anxiety and reward dependence, which indicates the extent to which such children value and are also motivated by the approval from others. **Don't forget that underneath the tough exterior of children with antisocial behavior is low self-esteem.** One important trait of antisocial children, and even adolescents, is that they appear to have no feeling, and apart from not showing care for other people's feelings or feeling remorse for hurting others, they also have a tendency of not displaying any of their own feelings except hostility and anger. These feelings are communicated by their aggressive acts. An analysis of antisocial behavior is that it's a defense mechanism that helps the child avoid painful feelings or prevent the anxiety caused by lack of control over the environment. Social learning theory actually suggested that negative behaviors are reinforced during childhood by caregivers, parents, and peers (Antisocial Behavior).

WARNING SIGNS OF BEHAVIOR PROBLEMS

There are several warning signs parents and caregivers should look out for that indicate possible behavior problem in children. The Center for Effective Collaboration and Practice (2001) released a list of the warning signs, some of which include:

- Excessive feeling of isolation

- Feeling of being picked on or persecuted

- Social withdrawal

- Being a victim of violence

- Excessive feeling of rejection

- Poor academic performance or low interest in school

- Patterns of impulsive and chronic hitting

- Expression of violence in writing and drawing

- Intimidating and bullying behaviors

- Uncontrolled anger

Some of the risk factors for antisocial behavior in children include:

- Unstable, violent, or tumultuous home life

- Genetics and family history

- School and neighborhood environment

- Poor and negative parenting practices

- Hyperactivity and neurological problems

It has also been discovered that youths with attention deficit hyperactivity disorder (ADHD) have been identified to be at a higher risk of developing antisocial behavior (Scaccia, 2016).

Child Behavior and Genetic Factors

The influence of genetic factors on development and behavior has actually been greatly emphasized recently. There is a growing body of evidence on the importance of the different types of gene-environment interactions and gene-environment correlations. Nature and nurture cannot be neatly separated in the way it was once believed (Bronfenbrenner & Ceci, 1994; Rutter, et al., 1997; Rutter, 1997). A very important message of genetic research is that genetic factors are not deterministic but probabilistic. Also, genetic factors and environmental factors, broadly speaking, are roughly of equal importance (Plomin & Rutter, 1998; Rutter & Plomin, 1997). There is sufficient evidence of a strong component in liability for attention span, prosocial behavior, and hyperactive behavior, the ability to inhibit behavior during infancy, toddlerhood, and preschool period (Rutter, Giller & Hagel, 1998; Thapar, Harold & McGuffin, 1998, Campbell, 1995). Cognitive deficits have also been associated with aggressive behaviors that are substantially heritable (Taylor, Sandberg, Thorley, & Giles, 1991; Taylor, 1994).

Effects of Parental Stress and Family Dysfunction on Child Behavior

Several family issues, such as unemployment and poverty, have great effects on parent-child interactions. It leads to an increase in the stress level of parents, which in turn impairs the quality of parenting and lowers the threshold of parental response to child misbehavior. Other family factors that have been related to children's aggressive behaviors include:

- Divorce
- Poverty
- Alcohol
- Substance abuse
- Single parenthood

- Maternal depression

- Reconstituted families

- The use of coercive and corporal punishment

- Poor parenting skill

- A parental history of antisocial behaviors

An increased level of aggression found even in toddlers is also found in abused children, and children from homes that have an occurrence of violence are more likely to exhibit aggressive behavior (Dodge, Bates & Pettit, 1990; George & Main, 1979).

The high exposure of children to media violence through movies, television, video games, the Internet, and cartoons has for a long time been associated with an increase in the chances of the children becoming desensitized to violence and behaving in an aggressive and antisocial way. It's important to note that there is inconsistency in the research relating to the use of violent video games with antisocial behavior, with findings of both an increase and decrease in aggression after exposure to violent video games (Gale Encyclopedia of Children's Health, 2017).

STAGES OF ANTISOCIAL BEHAVIOR

Three predictable stages of antisocial behavior have been identified. According to researchers, the first stage actually involves parents who fail to supervise, monitor, and discipline their children effectively. Inept parenting encourages children to avoid responsibility and work. The second stage usually takes place when these children who have been encouraged to avoid work enter school, where they may experience academic failure and social rejection. Due to the fact that they are deficient in social skills, such children will experience difficulty in figuring out what is expected behavior, and they will respond inappropriately and misinterpret social cues (Patterson, DeBaryshe, & Ramsey, 1989).

They usually have the ability to manipulate their teachers to avoid work, and they gradually start to perform poorly academically.

The third and final stage of delinquency usually takes place in late childhood or adolescence. At this stage, the child becomes a member of a deviant peer group that provides reinforcement for antisocial attitudes, rationalizations, and actions. The third stage ushers in the most serious delinquent acts and substance abuse (Patterson et al., 1989).

It was also reported by Patterson, Reid, & Dishion (1992) that the problem of children with antisocial behavior worsens as a result of the negative effect their problem has on their peers and teachers. A key developmental stage on the path of these children toward school failure and delinquency is their rejection by peers and teachers.

PREVENTING ANTISOCIAL BEHAVIOR IN CHILDREN

As previously mentioned, early intervention is key to preventing the occurrence of antisocial behavior in children. Schools have been encouraged by the Center for Effective Collaboration and Practice to develop and implement three different prevention strategies.

- **The Primary Prevention** - In primary prevention, students are engaged in school-wide activities that could deter antisocial behavior. Such activities address the following:
  o Emotional literacy
  o Anger management
  o Conflict resolution
- **The Secondary Prevention** - The secondary prevention targets students at risk of developing antisocial tendencies, engaging them in individualized activities such as:
  o Counseling
  o Specialized tutoring
  o Mentoring
  o Small group social-skills lessons

- **The Tertiary Prevention** - At this stage, students receive intensive counseling, which will help treat those students with chronic patterns of delinquency and aggression. Caregivers, teachers, families, and others need to coordinate their efforts at this stage to treat children with antisocial behavior (Scaccia, 2016).

There are also other ways of preventing antisocial behavior in children. The following points should also be noted in preventing the occurrence of antisocial behavior in children:

- Peer relationship with prosocial individuals
- Prenatal care and healthy nutrition
- Non-coercive methods of parenting
- A safe and secure family and social environment
- Early bonding with a healthy and emotionally mature parent
- Role models for prosocial behaviors
- Early intervention as soon as the problem is identified

These are all great ways of assuring the development of prosocial behaviors and extinguishing antisocial behaviors in children (Gale Encyclopedia of Children's Health, 2017).

It's important to note that the longer the duration of the antisocial behavior, the more intractable they become. Early occurring conduct problems, if left untreated, have a higher tendency to lead to the development of chronic antisocial behavior than if the disruptive behavior started in adolescence. *Although it is never too late to treat antisocial behaviors, researchers warn that if by the age of eight, a child has not been able to learn better ways other than coercion in order to meet his goals, the possibility for him to continue with his antisocial behavior throughout his lifetime is high* (Gale Encyclopedia of Children's Health, 2017).

Dealing with Antisocial Behavior

When treating antisocial behavior, the most important goals are to effectively measure and describe the child's actual problem behaviors and then effectively teach the child the positive behaviors that have to be adopted instead of the negative ones. Medication can be administered to control behavior in severe cases; however, it should not replace therapy. Children experiencing explosive rage respond to medication properly. However, an ideal treatment will involve an interdisciplinary team of social workers, guidance counselors, and teachers who will work with caregivers and parents to provide universal services that will assist the child in every aspects of his life (Antisocial Behavior).

In several cases, parents need intensive training on modeling, and they need to provide appropriate discipline to prevent inappropriate behavior, while also reinforcing appropriate behaviors in their child. Although there are several methods that could be employed to deliver social skills training, the most effective methods are systemic therapies. Systemic therapies address communication skills among the entire family or within a peer group of other antisocial children. This system works well because it has to do with developing or redeveloping positive relationships between the child and other people. The methods adopted in social skills training include:

- Token reinforcement systems
- Role playing
- Modeling
- Corrective feedback

Also, note that the success of the treatment is determined by the child's level of cognitive and emotional development (Antisocial Behavior).

Students at a higher risk as a result of difficult family and environmental factors may not benefit from school-based programs that teach conflict resolution, anger management skills, and emotional literacy. Such children will benefit from prevention efforts more individualized, which will also include social-skills training, academic support, counseling, and behavior contracting. School settings that have the capacity to deliver professional parental support and give feedback in a motivating way can also assist parents to properly develop effective parenting skills that will help interrupt further progression of antisocial behavior patterns in their children. At-risk children can get help from community-based programs, including recreational programs and youth centers with trained therapists (Gale Encyclopedia of Children's Health, 2017).

Parental Concerns

Although parents would love to get help for their children with antisocial behavior patterns, they may hesitate to do so as a result of fear that the child would be negatively diagnosed and labeled. It's important to note that almost all children would definitely engage in some form of antisocial behavior at various points or stages of development. In such situations, skilled parents will be patient and calm enough to lovingly confront their child and assist the child to identify certain behaviors that are unacceptable. In the event that these wrong behaviors continue or worsen, the behaviors should be seriously considered as precursors to more serious problems. For the sake of the child and family, early intervention is very important (Gale Encyclopedia of Children's Health, 2017).

Conclusion

Aggressive and defiant behavior is indeed an important part of normal child and adolescent development because it ensures their physical and social survival. Actually, some parents may show concern when they discover that their child is too unassertive and acquiescent. The level of defiant and aggressive behavior in children varies among children with age; for example, two-year old children will frequently engage in hitting, which will gradually decline as they get older (Moffitt et al., 2008). However, when a child exhibits high levels of antisocial behaviors by being disobedient and hostile, stealing, destroying properties, and becoming both physically and verbally abusive, it's likely the child is showing signs of antisocial behavior. Such cases should be treated as early as possible to prevent severe problems in adulthood (Scaccia, 2016).

CHAPTER 6

Juvenile Detention: The Development of Delinquent Behavior

Available information from research conducted over the past few decades on normal child development and the development of delinquent behavior indicates social, individual, and community conditions and their interactions are part of the factors that influence behavior. It is generally agreed that behavior that includes antisocial and delinquent behavior is the result of a complex interplay of individual genetic and biological factors and environmental factors, which starts during the fetal development and continues throughout life (Bock and Goode, 1996).

Although its obvious genes affect the biological development of a child, there is no biological development without an environmental input. This implies that both biology and environment influence behavior. Dealing with child delinquents is very important, not only because youngsters are committing serious crimes, but also because the tendency for the young offenders to continue their involvement in crime as adults is high. Delinquency is indeed linked to higher crime rates in adulthood and other negative outcomes. Actually, one estimate suggests 50-75 percent of adolescents who spend time in juvenile detention centers are later incarcerated in life, though the estimates vary depending on the measurement of recidivism and time period used (Nagin et al., 1991).

Did you know that one-fourth (24%) of all persons arrested for robbery in 2010 was under the age of 18? This is substantially higher than the juvenile proportion of arrests in other violent offenses, such as aggravated assault (11%), forcible rape (14%), and murder (9%). (OJJDP Statistical Briefing Book, 2012).

The propensity for criminal behavior actually starts much earlier than adulthood, and there is a need for early intervention at a young age. In order to prevent juvenile crime, it's important to first understand the causes. So, what are the factors that drive a young person to crime? Most of the factors that could drive a young person to crime can be complex, and in most cases it is a combination of several factors that interact with each other. Despite the fact that risk factors can help in identifying the children in dire need of prevention interventions, they cannot identify the specific children who will become serious or chronic offenders. Also, it's been long acknowledged that adult criminals were involved in delinquent behavior when they were children and adolescents; however, most adolescents and delinquent children do not grow up to become adult criminals (Robins, 1978).

RISK FACTORS

A great number of juvenile researchers have linked risk factors to delinquency (Hawkins et al., 1998; Lipsey & Derzon, 1998), and many have also identified a multiplicative effect when several risk factors are present. Based on a report by Herrenkohl and colleagues (2001), a 10-year old exposed to six or more risk factors is 10 times as likely to commit a violent act by 18 as opposed to a 10-year-old only exposed to one risk factor. According to Youth Violence: A Report of the Surgeon General (2001 [chapter 4]), The prevention of violence and violence intervention efforts hinge on the identification of risk and protective factors and determining at what point they emerge in the development. In order to be effective, such efforts need to be appropriate for a youth's stage of development. It's important to note a program effective in childhood may not be effective in adolescence, and vice versa. Therefore, the study of risk factors is critical to the enhancement of prevention programs. Identifying the specific risk factors that may cause delinquency for a particular set of youth and at specific stages of their development may assist programs in targeting their efforts in a more cost-effective and efficient manner (McCord et al., 2001).

There are several individual factors and characteristics that have been associated with the development of juvenile delinquency. Some of these individual factors include:

- Impulsivity

- Age

- Substance abuse

- Gender

- Aggressiveness

- Complications during pregnancy and delivery

There are some factors that operate just before birth or close to birth. There are also other factors that operate during and shortly after birth. It's also important to note that there are factors that can be identified in early childhood, while other factors can only be identified during late childhood or during adolescence. There is a need to study the development of the individual in interaction with the environment in order to fully appreciate the development of these individual characteristics in relation to delinquency (McCord et al., 2001).

Let's take a look at some individual factors associated with the development of juvenile delinquency.

PRENATAL AND PERINATAL FACTORS

There are many studies that have found an association between prenatal and perinatal complications and later criminal behavior (Kandel et al., 1989; Kandel & Mednick, 1991; Raine et al., 1994). Both factors represent a host of latent and manifest conditions that influence subsequent development. When it comes to prenatal factors, it has to do with a broad variety of conditions that take place before birth through the seventh month of gestation (Kopp & Krakow, 1983). Perinatal factors include health conditions such as poor breathing and severe respiratory distress syndrome. Despite the fact that these are risk factors, factors such as low premature birth and birth weight do not really lead to problems in development. Prenatal and perinatal risk factors may actually be able to compromise the nervous system, which will create vulnerabilities in the child and result in abnormal behavior. It's also important to note that children having prenatal and perinatal complications living in deviant, impoverished, and abusive environments will face added difficulties (McCord et al., 2001).

AGE

Based on studies of criminal activity by age, it has been consistently discovered that the rates of offending start to rise in preadolescence (early adolescence), reach a peak in late adolescence, and fall through young adulthood (Farrington, 1986a; National Research Council, 1986). Although the specific age of onset, peak, and desistance varies by offense, with time the general pattern has been remarkably consistent in different countries, both for official and self-reported data. A longitudinal study of a sample of boys in London (Cambridge Longitudinal Study) discovered an eightfold increase in the number of boys convicted of delinquent behavior from age 10 to 17, which was followed by a decrease to a quarter of the maximum by age 24. There was also an increase in the number of self-reported offenses in the same sample between ages 15 and 18, which sharply dropped by age 24 (Farrington, 1983; 1986a).

PSYCHOLOGICAL AND MENTAL CHARACTERISTICS

There are many individual-specific characteristics linked to delinquency. According to Tremblay and LeMarquand (2001:141), "the best social behavior characteristic to predict delinquent behavior before the age of 13 appears to be aggression," and based on the review of several studies by Hawkins and colleagues (1998:113), it was reported that "a positive relationship exists between impulsivity and risk taking, hyperactivity, attention problems, and later violent behavior." Also, delayed language development and low verbal IQ have both been associated with delinquency, and these links actually remain even after controlling for race and class (Moffitt, Lynam, & Silva, 1994; Seguin et al., 1995). It was also noted by Herrenkohl et al., (2001:223) that children with a low commitment to school, low academic performance, and low educational aspirations during elementary and middle school grades are at a higher risk of child delinquency than other children.

SOCIAL FACTORS

There are many social factors that could lead to the development of child delinquency.

THE FAMILY STRUCTURE

Several family characteristics, such as family size, poor parenting skills, antisocial parents, child maltreatment and home discord are associated with juvenile delinquency (Derzon & Lipsey, 2000; Wasserman & Seracini, 2001). A study of 250 boys by McCord (1979) discovered that among boys at the age 10, the strongest predictors of later convictions for violent offenses were poor parental supervision; parental aggression, which includes harsh and punitive discipline; and parental conflict. Research has indicated children from families with four or more children have a higher chance of offending (Wasserman et al., 2001; West & Farrington, 1973).

Historically, an aspect of family structure that has attracted a great deal of attention as a major risk factor for delinquency is growing up in homes that have witnessed separation or divorce. Despite the fact that many studies found an association between broken homes and delinquency (Farrington & Loeber, 1999; Rutter & Giller, 1983; Wells & Rankin, 1991; Wilson & Herrnstein, 1985), there is also a debate regarding the meaning of the association. However, it's likely that the increased risk of delinquency, which is experienced among children of broken homes is associated with the family conflict prior to separation or divorce, rather than to family breakup itself (Rutter et al., 1998).

Another aspect of family factor that may lead to the development of delinquent behavior is family interaction. Even in two-parent families, children may not get the proper training, supervision, and advocacy needed to ensure a course of positive developmental. Some studies have discovered that poor parental management and disciplinary practices are linked with the development of delinquent behavior. Factors such as excessive, severe, or aggressive discipline, the failure to set clear expectations, poor monitoring and supervision of children, and inconsistent discipline predict later delinquency (Capaldi & Patterson, 1996; Farrington, 1989; Hawkins et al., 1995b; McCord, 1979). Patterson (1976) through his research indicates that parents who make use of idle threats or nag are likely to generate coercive systems where children gain control through misbehaving.

Consistent supervision, discipline, and affection help create well-socialized adolescents (Austin, 1978; Laub & Sampson, 1988; McCord, 1991; Sampson & Laub, 1993). Also, the noticeable reductions in delinquency between the ages of 15 and 17 years seem to be related to friendly interactions between parents and teenagers, a situation that tends to promote school attachment and stronger family ties (Liska & Reed, 1985). The children who have suffered parental neglect actually have an increased risk of delinquency. Children who have been neglected were as likely as the children who were abused physically to commit violent crimes later in life (Widom, 1989; McCord, 1983). Loeber & Stouthamer-Loeber (1986) concluded in their review of several studies investigating the relationships between socialization in families and juvenile delinquency that parental neglect had the greatest impact.

THE INFLUENCE OF PEERS

There have been several discoveries from studies indicating that there is a consistent relationship between involvement in a delinquent peer group and delinquent behavior. For youths between the ages of 12 and 14, a major predictor variable for delinquency is the presence of antisocial peers (Lipsey & Derzon, 1998). According to McCord et al., (2001:80), factors such as peer approval of delinquent behavior, peer delinquent behavior, time spent with peers, allegiance to peers, and the pressure for deviance have all been linked with adolescent antisocial behavior. Conversely, it was reported that spending time with peers who actually disapprove of delinquent behavior may be able to curb later violence (Elliot, 1994). According to Steinberg (1987), the influence of peers and their acceptance and approval of delinquent behavior is significant, and such a relationship is magnified when the youths involved have little interaction with their parents.

There is a significant increase in the amount of time adolescents spend with their friends during adolescence, and peers also become increasingly important during this developmental period. **Peer influences also seem to have a strong relationship to delinquency in the context of family conflict.** For instance, adolescents' lack of respect for parents actually influenced their antisocial behavior, due to the fact that it led to increase in antisocial peer affiliations (Simmons et al., 1991). There is another research that suggests that adolescents often become involved with delinquent peers before they become delinquent themselves (Elliott, 1994b; Elliott et al., 1985; Simons et al., 1994). In cases where an adolescent was delinquent before having delinquent friends, the delinquency was exacerbated as a result of the association with deviant peers (Elliott, 1994b; Elliott & Menard, 1996; Thornberry et al., 1993).

COMMUNITY RISK FACTORS

The environment where youths are raised can greatly influence the likelihood of delinquency. Community factors can be divided into neighborhood and school policies.

NEIGHBORHOOD

Based on the available information from research, there is a strong connection between living in an adverse environment and engaging in criminal acts (McCord et al., 2001). Sociological theories of deviance hypothesize that disorganized neighborhoods have weak social control networks (which is weak social control as a result of isolation among residents and high residential turnover), and this allows criminal activity to go unmonitored (Herrenkohl et al., 2001:221). Despite the fact that researchers debate the interaction between personal factors and environmental factors, most of them agree that living in a neighborhood with high levels of poverty and crime also increases the risk of involvement in serious crime for every child growing up there (McCord et al., 2001).

School Factors

School organization and process play significant roles as risk factors. Schools where there are fewer teachers with higher student enrollment experience a greater degree of student victimization. Also, poor rule enforcement within schools is often linked with higher levels of student victimization (Gottfredson & Gottfredson, 1985). Although research on the relationship between school processes and offending is low, there is evidence to suggest that many school characteristics, including some of the points mentioned below, may be associated with antisocial behavior in children (Herrenkohl et al., 2001):

- Poor student-teacher relations
- Inadequate rule enforcement
- Low levels of teacher satisfaction
- The prevalence of norms and values supporting antisocial behavior
- Less cooperation among teachers
- Poorly defined rules and expectations for conduct

The impact of school policies regarding grade retention, expulsion, suspension, and the school tracking of juvenile delinquency was reviewed by the Institute of Medicine and National Research Council (2013).

They reported that such policies, which disproportionately affect minorities, have a negative impact on at-risk youth (McCord et al., 2001). **For instance, it was discovered that suspension and expulsion do not seem to reduce undesirable behavior, and both are actually linked to increased delinquent behavior.** Also, a cross-sectional study of primary and secondary schools in England discovered that large schools with formal and severe punishment structures in place actually had more cases of students misbehaving (Heal, 1978).

THE INFLUENCE OF THE ENVIRONMENT

There are other aspects of the environment that have been examined to be factors that may influence the risk of offending and some of these factors include the availability of guns, drug markets, and the impact of violence in the media. There is no doubt that the presence of illegal drug markets increases the chances for violence, especially at the points where the drugs are exchanged for money (Haller, 1989).

EFFECTIVE TIPS FOR PREVENTING DELINQUENT BEHAVIOR

Having discussed several risk factors that could lead to delinquent behavior, let's take a look at some effective ways of preventing delinquency.

PROTECTIVE FACTORS

Although there is no magic solution that will help prevent delinquency, understanding and building protective factors is one great way to start. So what are protective factors? According to the Center for the Study of Social Policy and the Administration on Children, Youth, and Families (2013), they are traits or experiences that help counteract risk factors, and these protective factors may actually reduce the chances of delinquent behavior. Take a look at some of these factors:

- **Social Connectedness** - Connections to institutions and people assist youth to increase in knowledge and skills, gives them a sense of belonging, and helps them find meaning in their lives (CSSP, n.d., 2013). Some of the signs of social connectedness include:

  o Friends who disapprove of antisocial behavior

  o Warm and supportive relationships with parents and other people

  o Attending religious services

  o Extracurricular activities, positive school climate, and commitment to school

- **Youth Resilience** - Resilience can be defined as the process of managing stress and functioning well, even when dealing with trauma and adversity (CSSP, n.d., 2013). The following are hallmarks of youth resilience:

  o Positive view of self

  o A sense of empowerment

  o Trust in others

  o Hopefulness

  o Realistic belief in one's ability to succeed

  o Spirituality

  o A sense of purpose

  o Taking responsibility for oneself

  o Positive future orientation

  o Motivation

- **Cognitive and Social-Emotional Competence** - Being able to develop competence in these areas builds the foundation for developing an independent identity and having a responsible, productive, and satisfying adulthood. Some of the signs that indicate a youth has cognitive and social-emotional competence include:

o Self-esteem

o Kindness to oneself, especially when confronted with personal suffering and failings

o Thinking about the consequences of one's behavior

o A belief in one's ability to succeed

o Spirituality (CSSP, n.d.).

• **Concrete Support** - Youth in foster care greatly need strong support and services that will help address their needs and help them minimize stress. This concrete support can be obtained when foster parents, social workers, and others take the right steps to make sure they receive basic necessities and specialized academic, health, mental health, psycho educational, legal, and/or employment services (CSSP, n.d.).

If you are caring for a youth or a child who has risk factors for delinquency, consider the following points.

Be very clear about rules and expectations

Explain in a friendly but clear way to your children at home what you expect of them, and always hold family members accountable respectfully and consistently. Ensure that you respond to misbehavior in a proportionate manner.

Build a connection with your child

Although building a strong relationship takes time and effort, it really pays great dividends. It's important to note that a caring and supportive relationship with an adult is the single most vital protective factor for children who may have experienced maltreatment.

ALWAYS KNOW WHERE YOUR CHILDREN ARE AND WHO THEY ARE WITH

Endeavor to make your home a place your child's friends would want to be. When you do this, you will be able to monitor what's happening and know their friends.

DEVELOP YOUR BEHAVIOR MANAGEMENT SKILLS

As a result of past trauma, children in foster care may have difficulty behaving properly, and educating them on how to manage their own behavior will help them succeed in life and stay out of trouble.

SEEK HELP

Always engage in frequent and candid conversations with your child's social worker about parenting success and concerns. Definitely, they want your child to stay out of trouble, and supporting you is a great way to achieve such a goal.

LEARN AND UNDERSTAND ADOLESCENT DEVELOPMENT

What you know will definitely affect how you interpret teen behavior and the way you respond. It's therefore very important you expand your knowledge, because there are recent advances in the fields of neuroscience and developmental psychology (Jones et al., 2014).

CONCLUSION

There is no doubt that preventing delinquency is a complex problem with no simple solution. However, risk analysis helps us determine the possibility of a youth becoming delinquent. Risk factor analysis also enables practitioners to create prevention programs that will suit the unique needs of individual youth and community. Protective factors are experiences that help counteract risk factors, and one of the best ways to support a youth's protective factors and prevent them from engaging in activities they need to avoid is providing them with extra-curricular activities. Parents and caregivers should try as much as possible to engage their children with positive activities rather than allow them to be influenced negatively by peer pressure and other factors (Center for the Study of Social Policy and the Administration on Children, Youth and Families, 2013).

CHAPTER 7

The Effects of Juvenile Incarceration, Justice, and Disparities

The United States has the highest rate of youth incarceration than any other country in the world through juvenile courts and its adult criminal justice system. In 2010, approximately 70,800 juveniles were incarcerated in youth detention facilities alone while about 500,000 youths are brought to detention centers yearly and this data does not reflect the juveniles that are tried as adults (Prison Policy Initiative 2013).

Presently, all states have adopted certain mechanisms to try juveniles in adult criminal court. The judicial waiver authorizes juvenile courts to waive jurisdiction over some criminal cases that involve minors in order for them to be prosecuted as adults in criminal courts. Also, in 15 U.S states, some laws give prosecutors the choice of whether to prosecute juveniles that are charged with certain felonies in juvenile court or criminal court. These statutes had a serious impact on the U.S juvenile justice system because the initial reason for establishing a separate juvenile court was to ensure that adolescents are kept out of adult prisons, from poor role models, and also limit their exposure to criminal activity. It was also adapted to provide interventions that are aimed at diverting them from engaging in further anti-social behavior and toward more positive outcomes. It's important to know that factors like minor's age, maturity, family history, education and other developmental factors have little, if any, impact on the sentencing of juvenile offenders that are convicted in a criminal court (Griffin, 2007).

PROFILE OF YOUTHS IN CUSTODY

A report provided by the Federal Office of Juvenile Justice and Delinquency Prevention and the U.S Department of Justice which is titled "Survey of Youth in Residential Placement: Youth Needs and Services," provided an in-depth analysis and profile of juveniles in custody. The survey used data obtained from over 7,000 youths in custody during interviews, and the following data was gathered:

- According to the report, 70 percent of youths in custody indicated that something very terrifying or bad happened to them during the course of their lives

- 67 percent of the youths reported experiencing someone injured severely or killed

- 26 percent of all youths surveyed stated that it felt as if life wasn't worth living

- Also, 22 percent of them reported attempting suicide at some point in their lives

- A total of 84 percent of them said they had taken marijuana, compared to 30 percent, which is the rate of their peers in the general population

- The report indicated that 30 percent of the youths said they used crack or cocaine, compared to the general population which is around 6 percent. Based on the report, there was a significant gap between the profiles of boys and girls

- While 63 percent of the girls were reported as having anger management problems, 47 percent of boys did

- Also, 49 percent of the girls reported experiencing hallucinatory experiences while 16 percent of the boys did

- While 37 percent of the girls reported having suicidal thoughts and feelings, only 18 percent of the boys did

According to the justice department, the facilities provided to treat such youths were inadequate in some core areas. In fact, among the youths that reported four or more recent problems related to substance abuse, only 60 percent of them said they had received substance abuse counseling in their current facility. Also, many youths in custody reported that they were having attention problems and difficulties in school. The total learning time of 45 percent of the youths was six hours or more daily, which implies that the youths had a learning time that's below that of the general population (Sedlak & McPherson, 2010).

Facts about Juvenile Detention and Corrections

Take a look at some facts about juvenile detention in the United States:

- Do you know that on any given day, more than 70,000 juvenile offenders don't live in their homes, rather, they are held in residential placement such as correction facilities, juvenile detention facilities, or group homes?

- After they are arrested, many youths are also detained in a residential or detention facility to await a hearing in an adult or juvenile court; this depends on how they were charged. Also, while the youths are in out-of-home placement, they are separated from their normal day-to-day life and community — jobs, school, family, and so on. In fact, there are more than 20,000 youths detained in America daily.

- It might interest you to know that 1 out of every five youth (21%) brought before the court as having a delinquency case is detained.

- The detention facilities are meant to temporarily accommodate youths that are likely to skip their court date or commit another crime before their trial. However, many of the youths that are kept in the 591 detention centers in the

United States don't meet these criteria, therefore they should not be there.

- Most of the detained youths are held in locked "secure" settings like a juvenile detention facility, and 83 percent of these youths are confined by at least three or more locks during the day (OJJDP, 2011; Holman et al., 2006; Sedlak et al., 2010; Sickmund et al., 2011; OJJDP, May 2011).

RACIAL DISPARITY AND JUVENILE JUSTICE

There exist major gaps in the level of involvement of minority youth, especially black youth when compared to white youth in the juvenile justice system. Over the years, the existence of disproportionate racial representation in the juvenile justice system has raised questions regarding the fundamental fairness and equality of the treatment of youths by the law enforcement bodies, court and other personnel connected to the juvenile justice system. Also, what happens to the youths as regards their dealings or lack of dealings with the juvenile justice system may have serious implications for subsequent development and prospects in future. The federal government has identified the disproportional confinement of minorities, and in 1988, Congress amended the Juvenile Justice and Delinquency Prevention Act of 1974. The Act required states participating in the Acts formula grants program to deal properly with the disproportionate confinement of minority juveniles in secure facilities. The states were expected to assess the level of confinement of minority juveniles and also implement strategies that will help reduce disproportionate minority representation where it was found to exist (Devine et al., 1998)

Currently, research and social policy on crime, race and the administration of justice in the United States are now encountering conceptual and methodological impasse. While some of the researchers and commentators tend to focus on racially disproportionate offending behavioral patterns as the cause of such disparity, others highlighted the persistence of biases among decision-makers in the nation's justice system. The suggestion that behavior versus justice system should be viewed as alternatives rather than as processes that feed into each other is narrow. The behavior versus justice system debate has been exceedingly narrow in their focus, and they have failed to take into account the key role that social injustice has played in the production of crime (Clarke, 1998; Lane, 1986; McCord & Ensminger, 1997).

LGBT and the Juvenile Justice System

There is no doubt that Lesbian, gay, bisexual, transgender, and questioning youths may present unique challenges in the juvenile justice system. It is evident from research that LGBTQ youths have a higher tendency to encounter certain environmental risk factors and barriers related to their sexual orientations and gender identities. For instance, when compared to their heterosexual peers and classmates, LGBTQ youths are more likely to be bullied at school, they are more likely to experience victimization and rejection perpetrated by their caregivers or parents—usually leading to these youths running away from home. Also, they are more likely to be homeless, twice as likely to be arrested and detained for nonviolent offenses and status offenses and also at a higher risk for illicit drug use. (Mitchum & Moodie–Mills, 2014; Friedman et al., 2011; Burwick et al., 2014; Irvine, 2010; Heck et al., 2014).

Although they vary, some studies have attempted to estimate the prevalence of youths identified as LGBTQ in the juvenile justice system. It's been estimated that LGBT youths represent around 5-7 percent of the total youth population of the nation; however, they make up 13 % to 15 % of those that are currently in the juvenile justice system (Hunt & Moodie-Mills, 2012; Majd et al., 2009).

Juvenile Incarceration and Mental Illness

It might interest you to know that between 65 percent and 70 percent of the children and adolescents that are arrested yearly in the United States have a mental health disorder. In fact, one in five juveniles has a mental illness that's so severe that it impairs their ability to function as young persons and also grow into responsible adults.

Without proper treatment of a child with mental illness, the child or juvenile may embark on the path of delinquency and ultimately end up in adult crime. The effective assessment of and also comprehensive responses in court-involved juveniles having mental health needs can effectively help in breaking this cycle and also produce healthier young people that are less likely to act wrongly and commit crimes. American teenagers experience conduct, anxiety, mood, and substance abuse disorders; however, a majority of them often have more than one disorder and the most common "co-occurrence" happens to be substance abuse with mental illness. Often, these disorders put children at risk for problem behavior and delinquent acts (National Conference of State Legislatures).

Behavioral disorders are usually characterized by actions that harm or disturb other people, and that can also cause distress or disability. Conduct disorders and Attention Deficit Hyperactivity Disorder (ADHD) are two major youth behavioral disorders. The Center for Disease Control estimated that around 9-10 percent of approximately 5.4 million American children suffer from ADHD. About 4.8 percent of the children take medication for their condition. The Center for Mental Health Service estimates that 1 in every 33 children and 1 in 8 adolescents have been affected by depression which is a potentially serious mood disorder that has afflicted many adults. It's important to note that the occurrence of depression in juvenile offenders is remarkably higher than among young people. Also, adolescence happens to be a unique developmental period that's mainly charac-terized by change and growth, and this makes disorder in teens more prone to change and interruptions (National Conference of State Legislatures).

Therefore, it's important to ensure the accessibility of ongoing assessment and treatment for youths having mental disorders. Proper screening and assessment are crucial to the effective mental health treatment needs of youths in the juvenile justice system. Through screening, youths that need immediate mental health attention and further evaluation will be identified. Also, proper assessment helps those who determine risks, placement, and treatment of youths in the juvenile justice system to do a better job. The juvenile justice system has been challenged by the mental health and substance abuse needs of court-involved youths to appropriately respond with effective evaluation and intervention. One way to improve the care and treatment of these youths and get healthier results for families and communities is by getting them involved in an active partnership with child-serving organizations and the mental health community (National Conference of State Legislatures).

A New Way to Fight Juvenile Crime in Chicago

Kids are killing kids on the streets of Chicago, but now there's evidence of a way to prevent crime in the city and nationwide without stationing a cop at every corner. Amid growing national attention on Chicago's homicide spike, the University of Chicago Crime Lab coincidentally released a significant study on the success of a violence-prevention program aimed at youth in grades 7 through 10.

The researchers, who have found scant evidence of effective programs dealing with youth violence anywhere in the United States, were taken aback by the results of their detailed study of 2,740 low-income males in Chicago public schools. "When it comes to crime policy, there is a lot of skepticism about preventing crime through social policy," said Jens Ludwig, director of the Crime Lab. "There is simply not much empirical evidence of much that works. It's the same skepticism that prompted mass incarceration in all the states." "This program, however, suggests that violence is more responsive to targeted social programs than I had thought. There was an amazingly huge reduction in violence. It was a surprise to me. We really can prevent crime." The study was introduced at a high school of 700 students where nine students have been killed in gun-related violence that year (Warren, 2012).

Is reform working?

If reform is working, one should ask- why are kids in Chicago at the ages of 14 and sometimes younger or older using automatic weapons to kill other kids and adults in 2017? Juvenile crimes have been part of the increasing crime rate in Chicago. In the sixties, seventies, eighties, and nineties automatic weapons were unheard of, kids were not killing kids as much, although the murder rate was much higher in the seventies, it mostly involved older teens and adults committing these crimes. Many researchers have concluded that the high murder rate in the seventies was due to numerous factors, including guns, drugs, gangs, unemployment, poverty, poor education, fewer social activities and ineffective policing strategies. There appear to be many similarities with the current rise in crime and murder rates in the Chicagoland area just as it was forty years ago. While mass incarceration is wrong and debated in many judicial areas, one can, however, surmise that when the inmate's population dropped at the Cook County Jail and prison, crime increased. For example, the Cook County jail population has dropped by almost 2,000 inmates in the last few years, and the crime and murder rates have soared considerably. Ask yourself- are the reforms working for jails and prisons with early release from incarceration and little or no rehabilitation?

CHICAGO'S INCREASING CRIME RATE AND MISGUIDED REFORMS

> *"We are not incarcerating a bunch of harmless and sacks who are merely caught with a joint"*

> —*Heather Mac Donald, Manhattan Institute*

According to police officials, in Chicago ex-cons that are well-known to the police as having proven propensity for violence are set free from prison early or let off lightly by judges only for them to wreak havoc, once again, on the city. This cycle of violence has led to over 800 shootings in 2016, and according to former Chicago Police Department Chief of Patrol Eddie Jackson, the rate of shootings and murders can't be reversed until the criminal justice system starts to hold offenders accountable. Illinois is part of the states implementing the recommendations from Prison Reform Commissions to help reduce or possibly eliminate mandatory minimum sentences and also reduce prison populations by as much as 25 percent (Hickey, 2016).

In fact, in 2016 there were more than 700 murders and over 3,000 victims of gun violence that involved youth and adult offenders (Chicago Tribune, 2016). Many victims were innocent toddlers and senior citizens.

This movement to slash sentences and also release inmates is further given momentum by the controversial police-involved shootings that actually galvanize communities and protests by civil rights group and Black Lives Matter. However, reducing sentences of violent offenders places the police as well as law-abiding residents of the inner city at risk. According to researchers, laws that ensure robust prison terms for dangerous people help to keep everyone safe. According to a criminologist with the Urban Institute—Samuel Bieler, the punishment of criminals provides great value; however, it's important to think of how punishment can be used effectively. The threat of longer sentences does not possess a deterrent value but what is needed is an effective way to transition prisoners into the community (Hickey, 2016).

THE UNITED STATES JUVENILE JUSTICE AND DELINQUENCY PREVENTION ACT

The United States Juvenile Justice and Delinquency Prevention Act of 1974 provides funds to states that adhere to a series of federal protections which is called "core protections," while caring and treating youth in the justice system. Take a look at the four "core protections" of the act:

- Jail Removal — Jail removal disallows the placement of youths in adult jails and lockups except under limited circumstances

- Disproportionate Minority Confinement (DMC) — The DMC provision requires that states should address the problem of over-representation of youth of color in the justice system

- Sight and Sound — It's a form of separation protection that disallows contact between adults and juvenile offenders (This means that if juveniles are placed in an adult jail or lock up under the limited circumstances, then the law provides that the juvenile offenders must be separated from adult inmates)

- Deinstitutionalization of Status Offenders (DSO) — The deinstitutionalization of status offenders and non-offenders requires that runaway youth, truants and curfew violators cannot be detained in adult jails or juvenile detention facilities (Wikipedia)

EFFECTIVE WAYS TO HANDLE JUVENILE OFFENDERS

Juvenile delinquency follows a pattern similar to that of healthy adolescent development. That implies that children and youth follow the path toward delinquent and criminal behavior instead of engaging in them randomly. Based on research, there are two types of delinquents:

- Delinquents whose onset of severe antisocial behavior starts in early childhood

- The second one includes those in whom this onset coincides with their entry into adolescence

It's important to note that in both developmental paths, systems, families, and communities are offered the chance to intervene and prevent the onset of antisocial behavior and the involvement of the nation's justice system. Evidently, the best and most cost-effective point to stop the "cradle to prison pipeline" is as close to the beginning of the pipeline as possible. One of the benefits of early intervention is that it prevents the onset of delinquent behavior and also supports the development of youth's assets and resilience (Silverthorn et al., 1999).

CONCLUSION

Preventing juvenile delinquency offers a tremendous amount of benefits and also spares the nation's youth from the consequences of committing crimes because many adult criminals start their criminal activity as juveniles and the interventions that prevent delinquency have great potential to reduce adult crime. It can also reduce the cost of arrests, prosecution, incarceration, and several expenses associated with offenses. Research has suggested that the most effective community-based programs happen to be those that emphasize family interactions. Also, Multisystemic Therapy has not only helped to reduce recidivism rates, but also it has helped to reduce out-of-home placement rates for a range of troubled youths. It's a program designed to help parents effectively deal with their children's behavioral problems, which include poor school performance and their children's association with deviant peers. However, the fact that effective programs substantially go unused indicates the lingering gap between what researchers know regarding the causes and treatment of juvenile crime and the several policies and practices that have remained entrenched in communities across the nation (Aos et al., 2006; OCD).

CHAPTER 8

Youth Violence & Crime: Effective Prevention Strategies

Available data from research confirms that just a few juvenile offenders will remain lifelong criminals, and age has been established as one of the strongest predictors of criminal activities and antisocial behaviors. There is a rapid increase in criminal behaviors in late childhood, and this peaks in the late teen years. However, the criminal behaviors decline in the early 20s throughout adulthood. The relationship that exists between age and crime has consistently been bell-curved across western countries, though there are variations, depending on the type of offense and the year (Farrington, 1986; Piquero et al., 2007). One of the most visible forms of violence in the society is violence by young people, and the main perpetrators and victims of violence everywhere happen to be adolescents and young adults. Non-fatal assaults and homicide involving young people greatly contribute to the global burden of injury, disability, and premature death (Reza et al., 2001).

Youth violence harms the victims as well as their friends, family, and communities. The effects of youth violence are not just seen in illnesses and disability, but also in terms of the quality of life. New research in criminology, neuroscience, and psychology clearly indicates that young adults between the ages of 17-25 happen to be a distinct population overrepresented in crime and the justice system. In this age group, criminal behaviors, prison population, arrests, and recidivism rates peak, yet the response from the justice system is low. Targeted interventions for young people transiting from adolescence to adulthood are rare (Zeira at al., 2016).

The problems caused by youth violence can't be viewed separately from other problem behaviors. Young people who are violent tend to commit a range of crimes and display other problems, like:

- Dropping out of school
- Lying compulsively
- Skipping class regularly
- Contracting sexually transmitted diseases
- Driving recklessly
- Abusing alcohol or drugs

It is important to note that not all violent youths have significant problems other than violence, and not all young people having problems are violent (Youth Violence, 2001). Close links exist between youth violence and other forms of violence. For instance, witnessing violence at home or being abused sexually or physically may actually condition children or adults to accept violence as a justifiable means of resolving problems (Fagan et al., 1994; Widom, 1989). Prolonged exposure of young people to armed conflicts may likely contribute to a culture of terror, and this increases the incidence of youth violence (Gartner, 1990; Briggs et al., 1994; & Smutt et al., 1998). In order to develop effective policies and programs that will help prevent violence, it's important to understand the factors that cause the increase of the risk of young people being either the victims or perpetrators of violence.

Patterns of Youth Violence

The patterns of behavior that include violence actually change over the course of a person's life. Violence and other types of behaviors are usually given a heightened expression from the age of adolescence to young adulthood (Dahlberg et al., 2001). In order to formulate effective interventions, it's important to understand when and in what specific conditions violent behavior takes place as people develop.

SITUATIONAL FACTORS

Certain situational factors play a vital role in causing violent behavior among adolescence-limited offenders. A situational analysis that explains the interactions between the would-be perpetrator and victim in a particular situation describes how the potential for violence might result to actual violence. The situational factors include:

- The motives for such violent behavior

- Where the violent behavior occurs

- Whether other people apart from the offender and victim were present

- Whether weapons and alcohol were present

- Whether other criminal actions, like burglary, were involved that could actually be conducive to violence (Youth Violence)

The motives for youth violence no doubt vary based on certain factors, such as the age of the participants and other people present. Based on a study of delinquency in Montreal, Canada, it was revealed that when the perpetrators of violence were teenagers or people in their early 20s, about half of the violent personal attacks were motivated by the quest for excitement, usually with co-offenders, and half by utilitarian or rational objectives (LeBlanc et al., 1989). It's quite important to note that for all crimes, the major motivation switched from thrill-seeking during the perpetrators' teenage years to utilitarian, which involves prior planning, the use of weapons, and intimidation in their 20s (Agnew, 1990).

It was discovered by the National Survey of Youth in the United States that, generally, assaults were committed out of revenge, in retaliation for a previous attack or as a result of anger or provocation (LeBlanc et al., 1989). Also, according to a Cambridge study, the motives for physical fights depended on whether a boy fought with a group or alone. Usually, in individual fights a boy is often provoked, then becomes angry and hits his opponent, or it could also be to release tension. Generally, boys often get involved in group fights to help friends or because they are attacked; however, they rarely fight because they are angry. Group fights are more serious and often escalate from minor incidents that happened on the street or in the bars, and they are likely to involve the use of weapons leading to injuries. Such group fights also involve the police.

A very important situational factor that precipitates violence is drunkenness. According to a Swedish study, about half the victims of violence and around three-quarter of violent offenders were intoxicated at the time of the incident. This position was also confirmed in the Cambridge study, where it was discovered that many boys fought after drinking (Farrington, 1993; Wikstrom, 1985). It's interesting to note a trait common among young offenders that may make them more likely to get entangled in certain situations leading to violence is actually their tendency to be involved in a broad range of problem behaviors. Young violent offenders are generally versatile, rather than specialized in the types of crimes they commit. Violent young people commit more non-violent offenses than violent offenses (Miczek et al., 1994; Brennan et al., 1989). Based on a Cambridge study, convicted violent delinquents aged 21 years had nearly three times as many convictions for other offenses that are non-violent as for violent offenses (Farrington, 2001).

The Prevention of Youth Crime and Violence

Early Intervention

Based on the growing body of research, it's clear that the better and more cost-effective place to stop the "cradle to prison pipeline" is as close as possible to the beginning of the pipeline. Early intervention helps prevent the onset of delinquent behavior and supports the development of youth's assets and resilience. Although past approaches focus on remediating visible and/or longstanding disruptive behavior, it has been proven through research that prevention and early intervention are more effective. Also, based on research, it has been demonstrated that delinquency prevention programs are a great financial investment. For instance, recent research by WSIPP discovered that quality delinquency-prevention programs can actually save taxpayers about seven to ten dollars for every dollar invested, basically due to the reductions in the amount spent on incarceration. Early intervention not only saves human lives from being wasted, but also it helps prevent the onset of adult criminal careers, which will definitely reduce the chances of youths becoming serious and violent offenders. When this happens, it also reduces the burden of crime on the society and helps save taxpayers billions of dollars (Loeber et al., 2003).

Positive Youth Development

The Interagency Working Group for Youth Programs, defines positive youth development as follows:

"an intentional, pro-social approach that engages youth within their schools, communities, peer groups, families and organizations in a manner that's constructive and productive, recognizes, utilizes and enhances youths' strengths and promotes positive outcomes for young people by providing opportunities, fostering positive relationships and furnishing the support to build on their leadership strengths."

One positive youth development model actually addresses six life domains of relationship, work, health, creativity, education, and community. Two key assets all youth need are:

- Learning/doing
- Attaching/belonging

When the necessary services and supports are made available to help youth in the six life domains, it's definitely expected to result in a positive outcome (Butts et al., 2010).

RELATIONSHIP APPROACHES

- Another set of prevention strategies aimed at addressing youth violence and crime is by attempting to influence the types of relations they have with other people they interact with regularly. Relationship approaches address problems such as the lack of emotional relations between children and parents, the powerful pressures from peers to engage in violence and the absence of a strong relationship with an adult who is caring (Youth Violence).

EFFECTIVE PREVENTION PROGRAMS

An increasing amount of research is being conducted to determine which of the many existing prevention programs are most effective. Based on current literature, there is sufficient evidence to show that effective programs are those that seek to act as early as possible and focus on risk factors and the behavioral development of juveniles. Generally, the Office of Juvenile Justice and Delinquency Prevention recommends the use of the following types of community and school prevention programs: (Herrenkohl et al., 2001).

- Bullying prevention programs
- Multi-component classroom-based programs
- Mentoring programs
- Classroom and behavior management programs
- Conflict resolution and violence prevention curriculums
- Social competence promotion curriculum
- School organization programs
- Comprehensive community interventions
- Afterschool recreation programs (Loeber et al., 2003)

Cognitive Behavioral Therapy

Cognitive behavioral therapy is an effective way of reducing recidivism in both adults and juveniles. It assumes most individuals can become conscious of their behavior and thoughts and then carry out positive changes. Usually, a person's thoughts are the result of their experience, and people's behavior is influenced and prompted by these thoughts. Sometimes, thoughts may become distorted and fail to accurately reflect reality. It has been discovered that cognitive behavioral therapy is effective with substance abuse and violent offenders, prisoners, probationers, juvenile and adult offenders, and parolees. It's not just effective in various criminal justice settings, both in the communities and institutions; it also addresses a host of problems associated with criminal behavior. In cognitive behavior therapy programs, offenders improve their "means-ends problem-solving skills," social skills, cognitive style, self-efficacy, impulse management, critical reasoning, and moral reasoning (Landenberger et al., 2005).

Mark Lipsey of Vanderbilt University examined the effectiveness of different approaches to intervention with young offenders (Lipsey, 2009). In his review, he analyzed the results of 548 studies from 1958 to 2002, which assessed intervention programs, policies, and practices. He grouped the evaluation into seven categories:

- Skill building
- Counseling
- Surveillance
- Restorative programs
- Deterrence
- Multiple coordinated services
- Discipline

When Lipsey combined and compared the effects of the seven interventions, he discovered that interventions based on punishment and deterrence appeared to actually increase criminal recidivism, while therapeutic approaches based on counseling, multiple services, and skill building had the greatest impact in further reducing criminal behavior. When he compared the different counseling and skill-building approaches, he discovered cognitive-behavioral skill building approaches proved to be more effective in reducing further criminal behavior than any other type of intervention (Lipsey, 2009).

Also, Nana Landenberger and Lipsey revealed programs based on cognitive behavioral therapy are quite effective with both juvenile and adult criminal offenders found in various criminal settings, which include residential, prisons, community probation, and parole (Landenberger et al., 2005).

INDIVIDUAL PERCEPTIONS AFFECT BEHAVIOR

Attitudes, beliefs, and values no doubt affect the way people think and how they view problems. Beliefs can actually distort the way a person interacts with other people, view reality, and experience everyday life. Cognitive behavioral therapy can assist in restructuring distorted thinking and perception, and this, in turn, changes the individual's behavior positively. Some of the characteristics of distorted thinking may include:

- Poor decision making and problem-solving

- A hampered ability to properly reason and accept blame for wrongdoing

- Immature or developmentally arrested thoughts

- The use of violence and force as a means to achieve goals

- An inability of an individual to consider the effects of his or her behavior

- The inability to properly manage the feelings of anger

- A mistaken belief of entitlement, which includes the inability to delay gratification, ignoring the rights of other people and confusing wants and needs

- The tendency to always act on impulse, which includes the lack of self-control and empathy

These unproductive and detrimental beliefs, thoughts, and views can be addressed and changed through therapy (Yochelson et al., 1990).

COMMUNITY POLICING

Problem-oriented or community policing has over the years become a very important law enforcement strategy used in dealing with not just youth violence, but also other criminal problems around the world (Goldstein, 1977). Although it can assume any form, its core ingredients include building community partnerships and solving community problems (OJJDP, 1995). For instance, in some programs, the police work with mental health professionals to help identify and then refer youths who have experienced, witnessed, or committed violence (Marens et al., 1988).

Such programs build on the fact that the police come in contact with young victims or perpetrators of violence daily, and they are provided with special training and linked with mental health professionals during the early stage of the youth's development (OJJDP, 1995). It's important to note the effectiveness of community policing programs has been determined with its successful implementation in places like Rio de Janeiro, Costa Rica, Brazil, and San Jose. When the program was evaluated in Costa Rica, it was found that there was a decline in both crime and perceived personal insecurity (Buvinic et al., 1999; Jarquin et al., 1997).

THE CONTROL OF ALCOHOL

One effective community strategy that will help in controlling violence and crime is to reduce alcohol. Alcohol happens to be an important situational factor capable of causing violence. In fact, the effect of cutting down the availability of alcohol on the rates of crime was examined in a four-year longitudinal study conducted in a small provincial region of New Zealand (Kraushaar et al., 1995). The rates of serious criminal offenses such as rape and homicide and other offenses (offenses related to traffic and property) were compared in two experimental towns and four control towns over a study period. Although both types of offense decreased both in the experimental towns and increased relative to national trends in control towns, there was a significant decline in crime rates for two years in areas of reduced alcohol availability. However, it's not clear to what extent the interventions affected violent behavior among youth or how effective the approach might be in other settings (Youth Violence).

GENERAL STRATEGIES FOR PREVENTING YOUTH VIOLENCE

Violence could come in different forms; it could be sexual, physical, emotional, or verbal abuse. However, in all its forms, violence is usually perpetrated by someone known to the victim, and this includes peers and family members. The following strategies will help prevent violence.

- Promoting a home that is safe and supportive through the following ways:
  - Promoting connectedness between the community and family members
  - Increase in the capacity of caregivers or parents to raise nonviolent youth
  - Supporting and facilitating help-seeking where family violence occurs
  - Assuring and promoting chemical and alcohol dependency treatment for parents
  - Educating people about the benefits of restricting exposure to violent media and how to restrict exposure to violent media
- Organizing the community to increase protective factors and reduce risks, which can be achieved by implementing the following strategies:

- o Providing youth with opportunities to discuss and develop healthy intimate relationships

- o Strengthening community standards against harassment, sexism, bullying, heterosexism, violence, racism, and aggression

- o Strategically engaging the youth in development approaches

- o Reducing the number of people living with firearms that are loaded and unlocked in their homes

- o Reducing access to alcohol

- There is a need to advocate with systems to help address social conditions and improve system practices related to violence. Take note of the following points:

- o Train professionals to be able to identify and respond to violence and refer individuals for support

- o Advocate for more funding in order to expand financing and reimbursement for preventive and primary adolescent health services

- o Decrease the level of institutional racism and hetero-sexism, and then promote cultural respect, inclusivity, and competency

- o Advocate for policy initiatives to meet basic family support needs, which include income, food and nutrition, housing, prenatal, and childcare

- o The provision of housing and care for all youths who cannot live at home

- o Endorse and promote a comprehensive package of preventive health services for young people between 11 and 21 years

- o Ensure safe housing and neighborhoods (Best Practices to Prevent Youth Violence, 2003)

Protective Factors

One of the traits that allow an individual to make appropriate behavioral choices in the presence of several risk factors is resilience. It explains why someone can resist mental health problems, substance abuse, and criminal behavior even when the person may be exposed to great adversity and stress (Finley, 1994; Spekman, 1993). It's important to note the development or availability of protective factors that can aid youth in resisting the influence of risk factors promotes resiliency (Walker et al., 1996). A number of protective factors that can assist in deterring youths from developing patterns of antisocial and violent behavior have been identified by researchers. The protective factors can be classified as internal (the individual) or external, which has to do with the community, peer relations, family, and school (Brooks, 1994; Garmezy, 1993).

Internal Protective Factors

These factors consist of personal attributes that assist people to overcome risks. It can be categorized as either psychological or physical. Some of the psychological factors that may help provide protection against violent and antisocial behavior patterns include:

- The ability of an individual to be flexible during periods of change, such as a change in work schedule and school

- The ability to make use of humor in deescalating negative situations

- Having efficient and effective communication skills

- The use of a wide range of social skills (Benard, 1995; Dobbin & Gatowski, 1996)

The physical characteristics that include personal hygiene and good health can serve as protective factors for children and youth.

According to Brooks (1994) and Spekman (1993), resilience can be promoted by the ability to understand and accept one's limitations and capabilities and having a positive outlook on situations. Also, the use of coping and stress reduction strategies like music, painting, writing, and dancing are protective factors that greatly enhance resiliency by enabling an individual to express inner turmoil creatively and discover some order amongst confusion (Wolin & Wolin, 1994).

EXTERNAL PROTECTIVE FACTORS

External protective factors can be categorized in school, home, and community domains, and three themes involving external protective factors have been identified by resiliency researchers. These themes seem common to the domains earlier mentioned. They include:

- Positive and high expectations

- Caring relationships

- Opportunities for meaningful participation (Benard, 1995; Davis, 1999; Grotberg, 1995)

There are many factors in the home that can help promote these themes; for instance, the attachment to at least one person in the family who engages in proactive and healthy interactions with the youth represents an important caring relationship. Fonagy (2001) discovered children who were insecurely attached showed anxious and fearful behaviors and perceived the world as threatening, in contrast to children who were attached to an early caregiver. The caregiver could be a grandparent, sibling, aunt, uncle, or parents, and such individuals may give the youth a sense of belonging and purpose within the family unit and value his or her abilities.

CONCLUSION

Youth violence is a serious problem with lasting harmful effects on the victims, their friends, family, and community; however, the goal of youth violence prevention is actually to stop violence from taking place in the first place. Solutions are as complex as the problem, but the prevention efforts should focus on promoting factors that protect youth at risk while reducing the factors that place youth at risk for perpetrating violence. The prevention efforts should also address all types of influences on youth violence: the society, relationship, individual, and community. Presently, many prevention tools have been developed and implemented, and many have been evaluated and found to be effective at preventing not just violence, but also related behaviors among youth. Some effective and promising programs include The Community Guide for Violence Prevention, Striving To Reduce Youth Violence Everywhere (STRYVE), Blueprints for Healthy Youth Development, and The National Registry of Evidence-based Programs and Practices (NREPP), (CDC, 2017).

"They (youths) tell me how they are not scared to die, but they are terrified of the lives circumstance forces them to lead."

— Thomm Quackenbush

CHAPTER 9

Women's Pathway to Jail

The rate of incarceration of women in the United States has greatly increased over the years. In 1986, for instance, there were about 19,812 women in U.S. prisons and jails, but the number skyrocketed to 106,000 in 2005, representing a five-fold increase within a period of 20 years (Bureau of Justice Statistics, 2005). Also, the number of women incarcerated for a year or more increased by 757% between 1977 and 2004, and it's very important to note this is more than double the increase for men. There were 183,000 women in the United States jail or prison in 2006, and this is about three times higher than any other country (U.S. Census Bureau, 2006). Also, more than one million women were being monitored in 2005 by the justice system in either probation or parole status (Glaze & Palla, 2005). Considering the increasing number of women getting involved in the criminal justice system, there is definitely a compelling need to properly identify and understand the factors leading to women's involvement in crime. An increased insight into the psychological factors associated with women's criminal behavior will no doubt help in formulating strategies that will help reduce the tendency for women to get involved in criminal activity. The subject of female criminality was actually a neglected issue, because it has always been the belief that crime is predominately a male phenomenon and society has always viewed the world of crime as only a man's world. Initially, criminologists ignored female criminality, and attention to female offenders was only limited to three aspects:

- The analysis of the depravity of violent women

- A comparison that aimed to understand women's lack of involvement in crime that's related to men

- The studies of prostitution

The reason for the limited attention to female offenders is due to the fact that women are passive; the few women who are involved in violent crime must be sick (Curran & Ranzetti, 2001). In recent times, there has been an increase in the number of crimes committed by females due to factors such as discrimination in workplace environments and family life, the marginal nature of women and complex lifestyles (Islam and Nurjahan, 2013). Also, the impact of popular media has influenced female involvement in crime (Siegel, 2007).

Early literature on the subject of women participation in crime, starting with Sigmund Freud and Cesare Lombroso, actually claimed female criminals were just anomalies and displayed biological and psychological traits similar to those of male criminals. However, sociologists and criminologists employed other paradigms in order to explain female involvement in crime stressing that socio-cultural factors are important. They also emphasized that the role of gender in crime market mirrors the role of gender in our society. They are of the view that if gender gap in crime was due to biological differences between men and women, then it would not change over time and space, which has actually happened. We are no doubt aware of the emergence of the "gender equality hypothesis," and they are of the opinion that the reduction in the gender gap in crime with its variation in different countries, both urban and rural, was linked to the reduction in gender gaps in other aspects of life (Campaniello, 2014).

FACTS YOU SHOULD KNOW ABOUT WOMEN IN THE CRIMINAL JUSTICE SYSTEM

Women are increasingly being detained at extraordinary rates basically as a result of nonviolent, drug-related offenses. Over the past 30 years, research in the fields of health, substance abuse, violence against women, and mental health and practice in criminal justice has disclosed that women offenders encounter several challenges that are not just different from their male counterparts, but also play a major role in their involvement in criminal justice. Take a look at some of the facts about women in the criminal justice system:

1. Women generally pose a lower public safety risk than men; they often enter the criminal justice system for nonviolent crimes typically involving drugs or property. When women are released from incarceration, they have a lower recidivism rate than men, and this also applies to reconvictions, rearrests and returns to correctional facilities, either with or without new sentences (Williamson, M. S.).

2. Women's involvement in criminal behavior is usually linked to their connection with others. Women's relationships with their family, children, and others are usually important to them, and an exposure to dysfunctional and abusive relationships in their lifetime can increase their risk for future victimization and the perpetration of violence. Also, women's unhealthy relationships with men or others often lead to their own involvement in crime and criminal justice (Williamson, M. S.).

3. According to the available data, women have been increasingly active in two categories of crimes: violent crime and property crime. In fact, women commit twice as much property crime as violent crimes (Bureau of Justice Statistics). According to the records of crimes committed by men and women in 2009 in the U.S., Italy and England and Wales, it was discovered that on the average, women tend to commit

more property crimes—particularly fraud, theft, and drug offenses (Campaniello, 2014).

4. Many girls enter the juvenile justice system having a troubling history of physical, emotional, and sexual abuse, and girls are more likely to be sexually victimized than boys while serving time in a facility. Trauma like sexual victimization has often been associated with mental health, difficulties in relationships and substance abuse, and it greatly contributes to criminal pathways for women. Incarcerated women with a history of trauma and accompanying mental health concerns are actually more likely to have difficulties with prison adjustment and misconduct (Ajinkya, 2012).

5. Women encounter further discrimination after their release from the prison. They face barriers in re-entering the society effectively, and this further hinders their ability to provide for themselves and their children. Some states actually impose statutory bans on people having certain convictions, restricting them from working in certain fields, such as child care, nursing, and home health care (Ajinkya, 2012).

6. Corrections policies and practices were to a great extent developed through the lens of managing men and not women. The policies and practices in prisons and jails do not reflect a good understanding of the risk and needs of female offenders, since a lot of the empirical research initially focused on male offenders only. A research study disclosed that gender differences were usually ignored in assessment and classification procedures for women (Williamson, M. S.).

7. Many women actually enter the criminal justice system with a disturbing history of sexual, physical, and emotional abuse. In fact, available reports show that 85-90 percent of women incarcerated or under the control of the judicial system in the U.S. have a history of sexual abuse and domestic violence. Some of the risk factors that contribute to women's criminal

behavior include spousal abuse, substance abuse, and mental illness (Ajinkya, 2012; Ney, 2015).

How Do Girls Get into Trouble?

This is a very important question, especially when trying to reduce the number of female offenders. According to some studies, both boys and girls tend to start their antisocial careers around age 15, the average age of onset not differing by more than six months across genders (Moffitt et al., 2001; Piquero et al., 2001). However, other researchers are of the view that females start offending when they are younger than males (Elliott, 1994). It's important to note that gender differences in the age of onset is likely to be most pronounced for aggressive or serious types of delinquency, while behaviors less problematic, such as alcohol or drug related offenses, have less gender-differentiated progression (Moffitt et al., 2001).

So What Is the Duration of Female Criminal Careers?

On average, males tend to have longer criminal careers than females but considering the difficulty in assessing when a criminal career is finished, the availability of convincing evidence of the duration of criminal career is sparse. According to a long-term study carried out by Roger Tarling, he observed a sample of female and male offenders born in 1958 through the age of 31 and found that the average duration for females was 4.9 years and 7.4 years for males (Tarling, 1993). A follow-up of the same subjects under study revealed that though the average length of criminal careers had actually increased to 5.6 years for females and 9.7 years for males, criminal careers were still remarkably shorter for females than males (Home Office Statistical Bulletin, 1995).

The Developmental Pathways of Criminal Behaviors

There are differences not only in typical progressions of offending behavior but also in the developmental course of aggression. Such differences actually emerge quite early, for instance, despite the fact that the typical disruptive behaviors of preschool boys and girls differ slightly, the behaviors evolve over time in strongly gender-dependent ways with the girls more quickly outgrowing such behaviors than boys (Keenan et al., 2003; Loeber et al., 1997). Girls are generally less likely than boys to be physically aggressive; however, by adolescence, the possibility for girls to direct their aggression at romantic partners, family members as well as at familiar females increases and becomes greater than that of males (Heide, 2003; Björkqvist et al., 1992).

Based on a detailed investigation using the data obtained from six sites and three countries, Lisa Broidy and her colleagues studied the evolution of physical aggression and other problem behaviors that exist during childhood in order to properly predict violent and nonviolent offending outcomes in adolescence. They observed that boys were more physically aggressive than girls during their childhood, however, the trajectories of their aggression looked similar. The trajectories of aggression began to diverge as boys and girls entered adolescence. Problem behavior seemed to continue for boys from childhood into adolescence especially in behaviors such as physical aggression but girls generally displayed fewer links between childhood aggression and offending during adolescence (Broidy et al., 2003).

This difference may actually be attributed to low base rate of offending outcomes among females or an indication of gender differences in trajectories of offending. It has been observed that early aggression is a robust correlation of adolescent aggression in males; however, it's much less an effective predictor of adolescent female aggression (Piquero et al., 2001). Although the evidence regarding the relative ages at which boys and girls are most likely to start offending is mixed, female offending careers have a tendency to be shorter than males. *Ironically, the shorter female offending careers result in a considerable damage in the offender's adulthood, which includes persistent behavioral and emotional problems that are usually more detrimental than those experienced by persistent male offenders* (Elizabeth, 2008).

THE NEGATIVE EFFECTS OF FEMALE OFFENDING

The negative effects of female offending goes well beyond the immediate consequences of their behavior, the cost of the behavior, and the cost of juvenile justice system intervention. According to a review of 20 studies carried out on the adult lives of antisocial adolescent girls, the following issues were discovered:

1. There was a higher mortality rate

2. The adolescent girls had poor educational achievement

3. A variety of psychiatric problems were discovered

4. They have dysfunctional and violent relationships

5. They have a less stable work history than non-delinquent girls (Pajer, 1998)

According to Moffitt et al. (2001), it was discovered that girls diagnosed with conduct disorder have a higher tendency as adults to suffer from a wide range of problems than those without such diagnosis. Some of the problems they experience include reliance on social assistance, victimization by as well as violence toward their partners, poorer physical health, and greater symptoms of mental illness. According to data gathered over a period of years, antisocial behavior among young people actually predicts school dropout; however, there is also evidence to suggest that there is a high dropout rate among aggressive girls (Stack et al., 2005).

Considering the available data from the Ohio Serious Offender Study, there are indications that only 16.8 percent of females that were incarcerated are high school graduates (Giordano et al., 2004). This implies that antisocial women tend to have lower occupational status later in life, rely greatly on welfare than non-offenders, and experience frequent job changes (Pulkkinen et al., 1993). **It's important to note that regardless of gender, adolescents with a history of antisocial behavior have a higher tendency to marry people who exert an antisocial influence or are involved in crime** (Moffitt et al., 2001). While there is a link between assuming adult responsibilities like child rearing and marriage and desisting from crime in males, this pattern is not common among females (Sampson et al., 2006; Moffitt et al., 2001). For females, the inverse happens to be the case; when they marry an antisocial mate, it reinforces their antisocial behaviors throughout their adulthood. Marriage for some females is also associated with increased crime and drug use (Brown, 2006). The marital relationship of female offenders may greatly experience instability and conflicts too (Pulkkinen et al., 1993).

Antisocial girls transiting to young adults have a chance of experiencing more relationship problems than their male counterparts (Moffitt et al., 2001). Although women are often victims of abusive partners in such relationships, they usually perpetrate abuse. In fact, according to measures of self and partner-reported violence, it was discovered that female offenders actually matched or even exceeded the male offenders' rates of partner abuse (Capaldi et al., 2004). According to the results of several studies, researchers have come to a conclusion that antisocial women inflict abuse that is serious enough to elicit fear or result in medical treatment that cannot be regarded as self-defense (Ibid.; Giordano et al., 1997).

Based on observational data from the Oregon Youth and Couples studies, females consistently had more tendencies to have initiated physical aggression than males (Capaldi et al., 2004). Such discoveries for females are quite notable since, among males, their adolescent antisocial behavior wanes significantly during adulthood. For female offenders, it appears that adolescent antisocial behavior is supplanted in adulthood by violent behavior in their home and against their family members (Robbins et al., 2003). Another point to note is that antisocial women are likely to reproduce at a younger age and usually with an antisocial mate (Moffitt et al., 2001). The result of such mating and reproductive tendencies is that young antisocial mothers and their children are left with inadequate financial, emotional, and social support. Also, early age parenthood can cause several challenges for anyone, and specifically, it can be problematic for early and chronic female offenders facing several challenges such as socioeconomic disadvantage, the increased risk of pregnancy complications, compromised parenting skills, and relationship violence (Stack et al.,

2005; Jaffee et al., 2006; Huh et al., 2006). There are several studies linking a history of maternal conduct disorder with unresponsive parenting (Wakschlag & Hans, 1999). **Particularly disturbing are data that suggest that mothers with a history of conduct disorder or aggression transfer at least three risk factors to their offspring, which include:**

1. Prenatal exposure to nicotine

2. Antisocial biological fathers (due to assortative mating)

3. Coercive or hostile parenting style (Zoccolillo et al., 2005)

In fact, the most common trajectories followed by female offenders tend to actually increase the chances that their children will definitely follow in their footsteps.

Conclusion

The recent changes that revealed the prevalence of female offending and the number of women in the care of the juvenile justice system have actually led many to believe that historically based assumptions and approaches to juvenile crime may need to be reconsidered. Women have increased their participation both in the labor market and crime market over the last 50 years. Although there is still much gender gap in the crime market, women involvement in crime is increasing partly due to the fact that other socio-economic gender gaps have been reducing. Presently, women have more freedom than in the past and with that freedom comes more opportunities for crime. (Campaniello, 2014)

Another potential reason for an increase in female participation in crime is as a result of technological progress and the change in social roles. Such advances and changes actually released women from home and reduced the marginal value of housekeeping. It's important to note that policies that will help to reduce the disparities between the skilled and unskilled female worker, like incentivizing female education, might lower the rate of crime among disadvantaged women. Crime among women can also be reduced by encouraging marriage and child rearing and the provision of family support policies. Analyzing the gender gap in the crime market and identifying its evolution and major determinants are important for effectively fighting crime. Although learning whether men and women behave differently in crime market is important, having an understanding of any differences that exist will help to uncover the main drivers of such differences and assist in setting policy incentives accordingly (Campaniello, 2014).

CHAPTER 10
The Causes of Crime in Adults

A question that has been in existence for ages—"why crime exists"—will never cease to be asked. Although there are many theories that attempt to explain this phenomenon, there are two specific concepts that stand out above others. It is believed that the social environment and biological traits that will eventually result in criminal behavior are the two main reasons why individuals commit crime. There is no doubt that the combination of both social and biological factors mold people into what they are, and this also determines the mindset of people that choose to indulge in criminal behavior. Based on the results of researches that were conducted regarding what really causes the criminal behavior in people, it has been concluded that both the environment and genes (biological factors) play a great role in the criminality of an individual (Jones, 2005).

There is a good amount of evidence indicating that our criminal justice system is indeed the home for people with psychological problems, and despite the fact that this may seem like a solution, it's actually creating a dilemma for our society. Labeling individuals as criminals creates a stigma for people suffering from psychological problems. **Some psychological problems have indicated to be heritable and when the right circumstances are provided, the individuals with the genes could actually find themselves indulging in criminal activity.** In the late nineteenth and early twentieth centuries, when the role of genetics was accepted widely, questions such as "should the society focus on limiting the reproductive capabilities of people suffering from certain psychological problems in order to better the society?" were widely accepted (Joseph, 2001).

During that period, prominent researchers believed that genes were completely responsible for criminal activity and criminals could easily be identified by physiological features. This point of view was also backed up by eugenics movement during the same period. This actually led to the act of sterilization that took place in the bid to rid the society of rapists, mentally disabled, and criminals (Joseph, 2001, p. 182). During this era, there was a remarkable inhumane treatment of people perceived as having antisocial behavior and a general belief that genes were the only factors responsible for criminal behavior. However, not so long after the inhumane practices of controlled breeding, there was sufficient evidence to back the idea that the environment actually plays an important role in crime. Based on the results obtained from early family studies, it revealed a predisposition to criminal behavior due to inherited characteristics and that a person's characteristics and personality could even be modified by the environment (Joseph, 2001).

So What Constitutes a Criminal Behavior?

Four general definitions were offered by Andrew and Bonta (1998), and they include:

- Acts that are capable of causing serious psychological stress or mental damage to the victim but affordable for the offender (this is known as psychological criminal behavior)

- Acts that are prohibited by law and are punished by the state

- Acts that are regarded as a violation of religious and moral code and believed to be punishable by a supreme spiritual being like God

- Acts that violate the norms of the society or traditions and that are believed to be punishable by the community

It can, therefore, be stated that a criminal behavior is any kind of antisocial behavior that is punishable by law or norms that are stated by the community. Based on that definition, it's obvious that defining criminal behavior is a difficult task since the acts that were considered as violations at one point in time are now being accepted by the community (Andrew et al., 1998).

The Relationship Between Environmental and Genetic Influences on Criminal Behavior

Several researchers usually gather information regarding genetic and environmental influences from three main sources: adoption studies, twin, and family (Tehrani & Mednick, 2000). The outcomes of family, twin, and adoption studies have been a source of great debate among researchers. While some researchers are of the view that these studies actually support the notion of a genetic basis for criminal behavior (Tehrani and Mednick, 2000), others concluded that there isn't sufficient evidence from the adoption, family, and twin studies to declare that genetics play a role in criminal or antisocial behavior (Lowenstein, 2003). Two studies were carried out in a bid to compare monozygotic (MZ) or identical twins and the rate of their criminal behavior with the rates of criminal behavior of fraternal or dizygotic twins.

These studies ordinarily were used to assess the roles of environmental and genetic influences, and if the outcome of the twin studies indicate that there is a higher concordance rate for DZ twins than for MZ twins in criminal behavior, it can generally be assumed that there is a genetic influence (Tehrani & Mednick, 2000). A study that was carried out examined 32 MZ twins that were raised apart and had been adopted by a non-relative shortly after birth. The results indicated that for both adult and childhood behavior, there exists a high level of heritability involved (Joseph, 2001). That study was important because it observed the factor of separate environments. Another researcher studied 85 MZ and 147 DZ twins and discovered that there was actually a higher concordance rate of the MZ pairs. After taking a look at the police report of the same twins ten years later, two other researchers concluded that there was a 54 percent heritability of liability to crime (Joseph, 2001). And within the same time of this study, two other researchers studied 49 MZ and 89 DZ pairs and didn't find any difference in the concordance rates. Therefore, they concluded that in respect to common crime, hereditary factors are of little significance (Joseph, 2001).

Adoptive studies are quite critical in examining the relationship that exists between adopted children and both their adoptive and biological parents mainly because adoptive studies assume to separate nature and nurture. There have been studies to test for the criminal behavior of the adopted-away children if their biological parents had indulged in criminal activity. The first adoption study conducted in Iowa looked at the genetics of criminal behavior. The researchers discovered that as compared to the control group, adopted individuals born to incarcerated female offenders had a higher rate of criminal convictions as adults. This evidence, therefore, supports the existence of a heritable component to criminal or antisocial behavior (Tehrani & Mednick, 2000).

The third type of instrument used in assessing the relationship between environmental and genetic influences on antisocial or criminal behavior is family studies. The research conducted in this field has actually been the least accepted by psychologists and other scholars as a result of the extent of difficulty in separating nature and nurture in the family environment. Children experience not just the influence of their parents' genes but also the environment they were raised in, making it difficult to assign the particular behaviors that were influenced by the two factors. However, one family study carried out by Brunner et al. (1993) is greatly acknowledged for its discoveries.

THE RELATIONSHIP BETWEEN WORK AND CRIME

The social significance and meaning of work and crime actually change remarkably over the life course. There seems to be a connection between criminal behavior and criminal behavior at various life-course stages. The meaning and the significance of work and crime witness a dramatic change over the life course; work may actually have one effect in adolescence while having a different one in adulthood.

Although it has always been stated that "an idle mind is the devil's workshop," new and emerging research findings suggests that the basic relationship between work and desistance from crime may be even more complex than earlier believed. Several counterintuitive trends at the societal level reveal complexities in how humans choose their path toward crime and employment. For instance, if work is closely related to crime, what could cause the continued decrease in crime rates during the great recession era of the late 2000s (Uggen, 2012)? Also, findings from new research is beginning to trace and specify the impact of being involved in the criminal justice system on future employment prospects, and this suggests a self-reinforcing relationship between the lack of quality employment opportunities and future criminal activities.

THE EFFECT OF WORK ON ADULT DESISTANCE FROM CRIME

There is a link between crime and work effects at the adult stage of the life course. Based on research, three major areas have linked crime and work for adults, which show in:

- The quality of the job, which matters in desistance from crime

- The relationship between aggregate unemployment levels and crime rates

- How prosocial bonds created through legal employment serve as a deterrent to crime

When considering its effect on crime reduction, the quality of a job actually appears to matter more than just the mere availability of legal employment (Allan & Steffensmeier, 1989; Sampson & Laub, 1993; Uggen, 1999).

Actually, a long line of studies reveals a relationship between high-quality job opportunities and diminished criminal behavior. Allan and Steffensmeier (1989) discovered that inadequate employment and unemployment leads to an increase in arrest rates among young adults, and Shover (1996) recognizes jobs with "a decent income" and providing the chance to exercise creativity and intelligence as aiding desistance from crime. Also, according to Uggen (1999), *it was discovered that former inmates who obtain high-quality jobs are less likely to reoffend than inmates who obtain lower-rated jobs.* Consequently, labor markets that are characterized by high unemployment rates and low-quality jobs are linked with increased crime even after statistically controlling for various sources of selection and background.

Crutchfield and Pitchford (1997) for example demonstrate that youths working in secondary labor markets have a greater chance to commit a crime when compared to those having higher quality and stable jobs. It has also been observed that professional networks that were developed through legal employment actually change the informal social controls that a potential offender is subjected to. *Adopting family and prosocial work roles and developing an identity as a law-abiding citizen are all involved in aiding desistance from crime* (Matsueda & Heimer, 1997; Uggen, Manza, & Behrens, 2004). For individuals with criminal histories, quality employment is usually in short supply though it really remains critical to establishing a prosocial identity during the process of desisting from crime (Maruna, 2001).

Aggregate-level examinations of crime and the rate of unemployment actually offer vital co-relational evidence, although the direction of the relationship is still subject to debate (Uggen & Wakefield, 2007). Economic choice and opportunity theories, for instance, predict that a positive relationship exists between unemployment and crime since individuals without legal income are forced into illegal means (Cantor & Land, 1985; Cloward & Ohlin, 1960; Ehrlich, 1973; Greenberg, 1985).

However, on the other hand, routine activity theory states that unemployed individuals spend more of their time at home, and this makes them guardians against certain crimes like burglary while simultaneously lowering the chance of their being victimized when they go outside their homes (Cohen & Felson, 1979). Cantor and Land (1985) have a different view; they posit that both processes work in tandem leading to a complex and difficult-to-observe link between crime rates and unemployment rates. However, it's important to note that empirical research discovered some effect of unemployment on property crimes specifically (Raphael & Winter-Ember, 2001), despite controlling for other demographic and economic factors; this relationship has also been less apparent for other criminal activities.

CONCLUSION

All through history, human beings have always attempted to provide an explanation of the causes of abnormal social behavior, which includes crime. In fact, human efforts to control crime date back to ancient Babylon's Code of Hammurabi, which was about 3,700 years ago. Then in the seventeenth century, European colonists in North America regarded crime and sin as the same. They were of the view that evil spirits possessed people who didn't conform to social norms or didn't adhere to rules. In order to maintain social order in settlements, individuals who exhibited any antisocial behavior were often dealt with harshly and swiftly. However, in the twenty-first century, criminologists focused on a wide range of factors in a bid to explain why people commit crimes, which included psychological, biological, social, and economic factors. Most times, a combination of those factors is the reason a person will commit a crime (JRank Articles).

The reasons for committing a crime could be pride, greed, anger, revenge, and jealousy. People make a decision to commit a crime and plan their actions carefully in advance to increase their gain while decreasing the risk involved. In such situations, these people consciously make a choice about their behavior, and in some cases they consider the life of crime to be better than a regular job based on the assumptions that crime brings greater rewards, excitement, and admiration—at least until they get caught. For others, they have a need for an adrenalin rush when carrying out a dangerous crime, and some commit crime on impulse, due to rage or fear. The human desire for material gains such as cars, money, and jewelry leads to property crimes like burglaries, auto thefts, robberies, and white-collar crimes. A desire for revenge, control, and power leads to violent crimes like assaults, rapes, and murders. In order to reduce the occurrence of such criminal activities, there is a need for proper punishment of those involved. It will discourage them and others from committing a crime. Effective punishment is supposed to make criminal behavior more risky and less attractive. Another way of reducing crime in our society is to make crime more difficult or reduce the opportunities. This can be achieved through better lighting, the presence of guard dogs, and a great improvement in technology, such as security systems (JRank Articles).

CHAPTER 11

LGBT Youth and the Justice System

Adolescents encounter several challenges while transiting to adulthood. Although most lesbian, gay, and bisexual (LGB) youth thrive happily during their adolescent years, having a positive environment that can assist all youth to achieve good grades and also maintain good mental and physical health is very important (CDC). For youths to live well in schools and communities, they need to be emotionally, physically, and socially safe and supported. A positive school environment has actually been linked to a decrease in depression, substance abuse, unexcused school absences, and suicidal feelings among LGB students (Espelage et al., 2008). However, according to a recent study that was carried out by the Human Rights Campaign, lesbian, gay, bisexual, and transgender youth face additional challenges that their traditional peers don't experience, and such challenges may have a serious impact on them. Some of the challenges that they face include bullying, exposure to physical and sexual violence, discrimination, and harassment.

According to a research by Garnette, Reyes, Irvine, and Wilber (2011), it was observed that LGBT youth are actually twice more likely to be homeless as a result of rejection by their family members; they either leave their homes voluntarily or they are forced out. That results in their homelessness which also exposes LGBT youth to the increased risk of victimization including rape, assault, and robbery. It was also observed that some of these youth end up engaging in "survival crimes." When they engage in survival crimes such as prostitution and theft, they also get exposed to the criminal justice system.

LGBT AND VIOLENCE

When compared to other students in schools, it was observed that negative attitudes toward LGB persons may actually position these youths at increased risk for experiences with violence (Coker et al., 2010). As earlier mentioned, the violence can be in the form of physical assault, bullying, harassment, and teasing. Based on the data from the 2015 national Youth Risk Behavior Survey (YRBS) of surveyed LGB students, the following information was gathered:

- 34% were bullied on school property

- 10% were threatened or actually injured with a dangerous weapon on school property

- 23% of LGB students who dated or went out with someone during the 12-month period before the survey was conducted had actually experienced sexual dating violence in the prior year

- About 28% of them were bullied electronically

- 18% of LGB students had also been forced to engage in sexual intercourse at some point in their lives

- 18% of LGB students also experienced physical dating violence (Kann et al., 2015)

Although it may be difficult to admit; LGBTQ people, including LGBTQ youth, can be both perpetrators of violence and victims of violence. Also, that violence frequently occurs in the context of romantic or sexual relationships. According to the Centers for Disease Control and Prevention (CDC), gay men and lesbians experience equal or higher levels of intimate partner violence (IPV) as heterosexuals, and it might interest you to know that bisexual women suffer much higher rates of intimate partner violence when compared to gay men, heterosexual women, and lesbians. Based on a CDC 2013 report, about 10 percent of high school students reported experiencing physical and sexual dating violence. Unfortunately, the majority of the studies of IPV among LGBTQ community focus mainly on adults, and even the studies of teen dating violence also fail to consider respondents' sexual orientation or gender identity. The limited data on LGBTQ teen dating violence is a cause for concern.

A study on LGBTQ teens that was released by the Urban Institute revealed significantly higher rates of dating violence among LGB youth than among non-LGB youth. The rate of sexual victimization for LGB respondents was actually 23.2 percent, which is almost double of the rate of sexual victimization for heterosexual youth that reported 12.3 percent sexual coercion rates. It's important to note that transgender youth reported the highest rates of dating violence having 88.9 percent reported cases of physical dating violence. The study by the Urban Institute revealed that LGB youth were actually more likely than their heterosexual peers to perpetrate dating violence (Human Rights Campaign).

LGBT YOUTH AND THE JUVENILE JUSTICE SYSTEM

Did you know that gay, transgender, and gender nonconforming youth are remarkably over-represented in the juvenile justice system? An estimate of 300,000 gay and transgender youth are actually arrested and/or detained yearly. A breakdown of the figures shows that 60 percent of the population are black or Latino. Although gay and transgender youth represent about five to seven percent of the overall youth population of the United States, they compose 13 to 15 percent of people currently in the juvenile justice system. The high rates of the involvement of LGBT youth in the juvenile system are due to the abandonment of gay and transgender youth by their communities and families and also their victimization in schools. **This is the sad reality that positions this group of people at a heightened risk of entering the school-to-prison pipeline** (Hunt & Moodie-Mills, 2012).

Based on research, gay and transgender youth that enter the juvenile justice system are twice as likely to have encountered child abuse, family conflict, and homelessness as other youth. Considering the fact that these youth greatly depend on their families to meet their needs materially, when they are rejected by their families, they become emotionally and physically vulnerable, especially if they find themselves on the streets with no support. Gay and transgender youth that flee abuse and hostility at home and in temporary placements have a higher tendency to end up homeless which happens to be the greatest predictor of involvement with the juvenile justice system. Actually, gay and transgender youth represent about 40 percent of the homeless youth population despite the fact that they make up generally about five to seven percent of the youth population. About 39 percent of homeless gay and transgender youth reported being involved in the juvenile justice system at some level. Homeless gay and transgender youth are more likely to engage in criminal behaviors like theft, drug sales, or survival sex, which increases their chance of being arrested and detained. They are also at an increased risk of detainment for getting involved in crimes that are related to homelessness, like sleeping in public spaces and violating youth curfew laws. (Hunt & Moodie-Mills, 2012).

LGBT Risky Behaviors

Unlike their peers, LGBT adolescents usually cope with their problems at school, home, or in the community by using alcohol and abusing other drugs. According to a study that tracked youth substance abuse within a period of three months:

- 69 percent of gay male adolescents reported the use of alcohol
- 26 percent used alcohol one or more times weekly
- About 44 percent reported the use of alcohol and other drugs
- Eight percent considered themselves to be drug dependent
- A total of 83 percent of lesbian adolescents reported alcohol use
- 11 percent reported the use of crack/cocaine and 56 percent reported the use of drugs (Langlois, M)

No doubt, youth that experience parental violence are also more likely to report cases of violence within their dating relationships.

It's interesting to note that dating violence during adolescence is commonly accepted as a precursor to domestic or intimate partner violence in adulthood. Teen dating violence victims are faced with greater risk of issues such as drug and alcohol problems, suicidality and re-victimization in young adulthood, and this is a problem that has actually been shown to disproportionately affect LGBTQ teens (Human Rights Campaign).

THE EFFECTS OF VIOLENCE ON EDUCATION AND MENTAL HEALTH OF LGB

The exposure to violence can lead to serious negative effects on the health and education of any young person. This may actually account for some of the health-related disparities that exist between LGB and heterosexual youth (Bouris et al., 2016; Huebner et al., 2015; Russell et al., 2011). According to the 2015 YRBS, it was observed that LGB students were actually 140% (12% v 5%) more likely to be absent from school at least in a day during the 30 days prior to the survey as a result of safety concerns when compared with heterosexual students (Kann et al., 2015). Although absenteeism has not been used as a direct measure of school performance, it has been associated with low graduation rates, which leads to lifelong consequences. Also, a complex combination of several factors can greatly impact youth health outcomes. LGB youth are at greater risk of substance abuse, suicide, depression, and other sexual behaviors that can actually position them at increased risk of HIV and other STDs (Kann et al., 2015). In fact, almost one-third (29%) of LGB youth had actually attempted suicide at least once in the prior year compared to heterosexual youth (Kann et al., 2015). Also, in 2014, young gay and bisexual men accounted for eight out of 10 HIV diagnoses among youth (CDC, 2014).

HOW SCHOOLS CAN HELP LGBT YOUTH

It's important for schools to implement evidence-based policies, procedures, and activities that are designed to enhance or promote a healthy environment for youths, including LGBT students. For instance, according to research, schools with LGB support groups such as gay-straight alliances have shown that LGB students were less likely to miss school because they felt unsafe at school, experience threats of violence, or even attempt suicide than students in schools without LGB support groups (Goodenow et al., 2006). Also, according to a recent study, it was discovered that LGB students experienced fewer suicidal thoughts and attempts when schools had gay-straight alliances and policies that prohibited the expression of homophobia in place for three years or more (Saewcy et al., 2014). The following policies and practices can help schools to promote health and safety among LGB youth.

1. The schools should encourage respect for all students and also prohibit harassment, bullying, and violence against all students (Hatzenbuehler & Keyes, 2013).

2. Schools should encourage student-led and student-organized school clubs that promote a welcoming, safe, and accepting school environment (For example, gender and sexuality alliances or gay-straight alliances, which are clubs that are open to youth of all gender and sexual orientations (Hatzenbuehler et al., 2014; Saewcy et al., 2014; Heck et al., 2014).

3. There is a need to identify "safe spaces" like counselors' designated classrooms or counselors' office where LGB youth can get support from teachers, administrators, or other school staff (Hatzenbuehler et al., 2014).

4. Schools should ensure that educational materials or health curricula include HIV, STDs, and pregnancy-prevention information that is also relevant to LGB youth such as making sure that curricula or materials make use of language and terminology (Hatzenbuehler et al., 2014; Mustanski et al., 2015)

5. School staff should be trained on how to create a safe and supportive school environment for every student regardless of their gender or sexual orientation, and staff should be

encouraged to attend such trainings (Hatzenbuehler et al., 2014; De Pedro et al., 2017).

6. Also, schools should facilitate access to community-based providers that have great experience providing health services, including social, psychological, HIV/STD testing, and counseling services to LGBTQ youth (Hatzenbuehler et al., 2014; Bauermeister et al., 2015).

So How Can Parents Help?

Obviously, positive parenting practices like engaging in honest and open conversations can greatly help to reduce teen health risk behaviors. The manner parents engage with their LGB teen can have an immense impact on their adolescent's present and future mental and physical health (Bouris et al., 2010). Parents that are supportive and accepting can assist youth to cope with the challenges of being an LGB teen (Ryan et al., 2010). Conversely, unsupportive parents that react negatively to the realization that their son or daughter is LGB can make it quite difficult for their teen to thrive. It's important to note that parent rejection has been linked to the use of drugs, alcohol, depression, and risky behavior among teens (Ryan et al., 2009; Puckett et al., 2015).

In order to be supportive, it's important for parents to discuss openly and supportively with their teen about their concerns and closely observe their teens for behaviors that might be an indication of their teen being a victim of violence or bullying or if their teen is victimizing others. Parents should take actions immediately when they discover that bullying, depression, or violence is suspected, they should work with school personnel as well as other adults in the community. Although there is need for more research to help understand the association between parenting and the health of LGB youth, parents can influence the health of their LGB youth by adopting the following research-based steps:

1. **Talk and listen-** When parents talk and listen to their teen in a manner that allows an open discussion about their sexual orientation, it greatly helps the teen to feel supported and loved. It's important for parents to engage in honest conversation with their teens regarding sex and ways they can avoid unsafe situations and sexual behaviors.

2. **Parents should always stay involved-** Parents that make an effort to know their teen's friends and also how their teen is doing can help their teen not only to stay safe but also feel cared for. Parents also need to continue to include their teen in family activities and events and ensure their teens feel supported. They should be able to help their teens develop an effective plan that will help them deal with their challenges and stay safe.

3. **Provide support-** It's important for parents to understand that teens find it quite difficult to share their sexual orientation. Parents that take time to come to terms with the way they feel about their teen's sexual orientation will definitely be more capable of responding calmly to their teen's sexual orientation and will be able to use respectful language. Parents need to develop common goals with their teen, which includes doing well in school and being healthy.

4. **Parents should be proactive-** Information is power. Parents can access lots of information and resources online and learn more about how they can effectively support their LGB teen, their teen friends, and other family members (CDC).

CONCLUSION

Societal factors like discrimination, bullying, and violence no doubt increase the health risks for anyone, but LGBTQ youth encounter elevated risks and associated negative health and mental outcomes. LGBTQ youth encounter several challenges such as bias-based bullying and harassment, rejection from family members and homelessness. However, not only do they experience violence such as hate crime from other people that are transphobic and homophobic, but also they experience violence within the LGBTQ community (Human Rights Campaign). Due to their rejection by their families, about 26 percent of LGB youth feel compelled to leave home and about 50 percent of gay males that leave their home early actually engage in prostitution in order to support themselves, which places them at a higher risk for assault, rape, HIV infection, and other sexually transmitted diseases (STDs), (Langlois, M). Parents, caregivers, school administrators, and teachers should endeavor to learn new ways of ensuring that LGBT youth do not feel victimized, bullied, and assaulted. Sensitivity at first contact is no doubt critical and also the conveyance of empathy and the provision of useful information regarding supportive community, and the instillation of hope will go a long way in ensuring that LGBT youth do not get victimized, bullied or engage in violence and criminal activities.

CHAPTER 12

Juvenile Mental Illness and Treatment

"Sixty-five to seventy percent of children in the juvenile justice system have a diagnosable mental health condition, and children in the juvenile justice system have substantially higher rates of behavioral health conditions than children in the general population. At least seventy-five percent of youth in the juvenile justice system experienced traumatic victimization, and ninety-three percent reported exposure to adverse childhood experiences including child abuse, family and community violence, and serious illness."

— (Baglivio et al., 2014)

The reliance on the juvenile justice system to meet the needs of juvenile offenders having mental health issues has greatly increased over the past decade. The juvenile justice system is currently faced with the task of not only providing proper mental assessments of youths but also providing effective treatment services for its youths. Originally, the juvenile justice system was both a rehabilitative and preventive approach that emphasized the various needs and rights of children over the appeal to punish them (Garascia, 2005; Statistics Canada, 2004; Sickmund, 2004).

The incarceration of a sizeable proportion of these children and adolescents is a result of violent, aggressive, and antisocial behaviors. There is evidence to suggest that aggression and violence are not actually the only problems that youths face and may not be the most serious. Based on research, there is growing evidence that the majority of youths and children within correctional settings suffer from one or more mental disorders (Abram, Teplin, McClelland & Dulcan, 2003; Andre, Pease, Kendall & Boulton, 1994; Uzlen & Hamilton, 1998).

Presently, urgent calls are being made to respond to the treatment and rehabilitation needs of children and adolescents within these settings because the mental health prognosis for many of them is poor. The general consensus across studies indicates the majority of incarcerated youths actually meet the criteria for at least one DSMIV disorder and about 20 percent of youths further meet the diagnostic criteria for serious mental disorder—a serious emotional disturbance leading to functional impairment (Cocozza & Skowyra, 2000).

HISTORY OF JUVENILE MENTAL ILLNESS

As observed by Garascia (2005), originally, the juvenile justice system was both rehabilitative and also preventative in approach, which emphasized the needs and rights of youths over the appeal to punish them. Based on The Juvenile Justice and Delinquency Prevention Act of 1974, the major goal of juvenile justice was to separate the youth from the formal punitive processing of the adult justice system, and this led to the use of community-based programs instead of larger institutions. There was, however, an interesting shift in the treatment of juvenile offenders in the justice system in the 1980s and 1990s. Before the 1980s, juvenile offenders were seen as rehabilitative; however, due to a surge in violent delinquency, this perspective was short-lived, and the protection of the community became the main goal (Underwood et al., 2016).

Consequently, a new approach was developed by the juvenile justice system that favors the punishment/criminalization perspective over a rehabilitative/medicalization perspective. Also, just like the zero-tolerance attitude of the education system during the early 1990s, over half of the states in the United States made revisions that enabled juvenile offenders to be prosecuted easily in the adult criminal court, and this was followed by punitive laws passed to address adolescent crime (Fried et al., 2001; Wald et al., 2003).

Although there has been a shift in the U.S. justice system from a punitive approach to a rehabilitative model of care, it was not focused on community-based provision of services but on youth corrections systems to care for the mental health and other specialized needs of juvenile offenders. As a result of this development, many juvenile justice systems were ill-equipped to properly deal with the acute needs of juveniles with mental health disorders. The United States Department of Justice (USDJ) has several investigations providing the evidence that mental health services for youth in juvenile justice is usually inadequate or unavailable (USDJ, 2011). Some of the barriers against the provision of adequate services include:

- Inadequate administrative capacity

- Insufficient policy development

- Lack of training for staff

- Insufficient resources

- Lack of appropriate staffing

Juvenile corrections personnel are seriously hindered from providing adequate services to youth offenders having mental health concerns due to factors such as lack of research, insufficient policy development, inadequate models of care, inadequate practice, and ineffective experience and training of staff.

JUVENILE MENTAL ILLNESS IN THE JUSTICE SYSTEM

The population of youth having mental disorders within the juvenile justice system has been found to be consistently higher than within the general population of adolescents. Based on estimates, approximately 50-70 percent of about 2 million youth involved in the juvenile justice system meet the criteria for mental health disorder.

Also, approximately 40-80 percent of incarcerated juveniles have been identified to have at least one diagnosable mental health disorder. In previous studies of juvenile offender detention facilities, two-thirds of males and three-quarters of females were found to meet the criteria for at least a mental health disorder, while one-third met the criteria for substance use disorder (Underwood et al., 2016).

Several comprehensive studies have revealed that certain types of mental illness are common among juvenile offenders, and some symptoms actually increase the risk of youth engaging in aggressive behaviors. It is also important to note that the risk of aggression increases for many specific disorders and comorbid disorders due to the fact that emotional symptoms such as anger and self-regulatory symptoms tend to increase such risk (Stoddard-Dare et al., 2011; Teplin et al., 2002; Wasserman et al., 2002; and Atkins et al., 1999).

Some common mental disorders found in youth offenders include:

- Affective disorders such as:
  o Persistent depression
  o Manic episodes
  o Major depression
- Anxiety disorders such as:
  o Panic generalized anxiety
  o Post-traumatic stress disorder
  o Obsessive-compulsive disorder
- Psychotic disorder
- Disruptive behavior disorders such as:
  o Attention deficit hyperactivity disorder
  o Conduct oppositional defiant disorder
- Substance use disorders (Underwood et al., 2016)

According to Heilbrum et al., (2005), understanding the link between youth offending and mental health difficulties is crucial when considering the treatment response because there is sufficient evidence to suggest that mental health difficulties are linked directly and indirectly to later offending behavior by youths.

Mood disorders, especially depression, occur in 10-25 percent of youths in the juvenile justice system, and the irritable mood that is usually associated with depressive disorders increases youths' chances of inciting angry responses from other people. This will increase their risk of engaging in acts that are physically aggressive causing them to get arrested (Grisso, 2008: Loeber et al., 1994; and Takeda, 2000).

However, the mood disorder of the adolescent may increase the risk of altercations with others while in custody or even increase the risk of anger at oneself leading to self-injurious behaviors. The high prevalence of juvenile mental disorders within the juvenile justice system does not actually require the need for treatment; rather, it emphasizes the urgent need for different levels of mental health care with various treatment options.

While some youths that meet the criteria for a disorder experience this disorder temporarily and only require emergency services, others with chronic mental health needs will likely require clinical care well into adulthood. Although some juvenile offenders will function well despite their symptoms, others may show limited functionality. There is a need, therefore, for an effective screening and assessment process to help deal with different individual needs and also provide varied effective treatment options. There is no doubt such tasks are weighty for just one system to handle effectively (Roberts et al., 1998).

JUVENILE MENTAL ILLNESS AND EFFECTIVE TREATMENT

Evidence shows it's beneficial to treat youth in acute distress as a result of mental illness. Many types of psychosocial and psychotherapeutic interventions are available for juveniles with mental disorders that focus mainly on youth having mental health difficulties and delinquent behaviors. Although there is limited evidence to confirm the efficacy of some of these approaches, some effective therapeutic models having promising evidence for their effectiveness in treating youth offenders are available, and some of them will be explained below.

FUNCTIONAL FAMILY THERAPY (FFT)

The FFT approach is a brief family-centered approach that was developed in the 1960s. It was developed in response to multi-need youth and families, and it's used for youth's ages 11 to 18 who are at risk for and/or presenting with delinquency, conduct disorder, violence, disruptive behavior disorders, substance abuse, and oppositional defiant disorder. Based on reports from the National Mental Health Association, a five-year follow-up study discovered that less than 10 percent of juveniles receiving Functional Family Therapy versus 60 percent of youth found in juvenile court had records for subsequent arrests. According to research, although FFT has proved to be an effective model for reducing recidivism, the training of behavioral health providers in the FFT model is essential (Shelton, 2005).

THE MULTISYSTEMIC THERAPY

The multisystemic therapy is one of the best available treatment approaches for juvenile offenders having mental health needs as indicated by empirical literature. It is an intensive multi-modal family-based approach that is suitable for treating identified causal factors and also correlating factors of delinquency and substance abuse. It is effective for treating juvenile offenders with emotional and behavioral problems. As demonstrated by studies, it has led to reductions as high as 70 percent in the rates of re-arrest and improvements in familial functioning; reductions of up to 64 percent in out-of-home placements; and decreases in the mental health concerns for serious youth offenders (National Mental Health Association, 2004).

MULTIDIMENSIONAL TREATMENT FOSTER CARE (MTFC)

It is an alternative to residential, secure-care, group, or hospitalization treatment process for adolescents having severe and chronic emotional and behavioral disorders. This type of care allows adolescents to be placed with trained local and supervised families for about six to nine months. During the MTFC placement, family therapy is carried out. The National Mental Health Association research about the program has indicated that youth juvenile offenders spent 60 percent fewer days incarcerated than those that did not receive the services, and they also had significantly fewer arrests. Multidimensional Treatment Foster Care has also proven to be effective for non-targeted outcomes like completion of homework, pregnancy, and school attendance. The treatment approach was found to decelerate girl's depressive symptoms and provide greater benefits for girls having higher levels of initial depressive symptoms (Leve et al., 2007; Harold et al., 2013).

Diversion

The Mental Health America is of the view that most youths do not need to be incarcerated. Rather, as much as possible, the children should be diverted away from the juvenile justice system toward community-based services and behavioral health treatment where needed—especially for technical probation violations and non-violent offenses. The treatment of children having behavioral health conditions is most effective when properly planned and integrated at the local level with other effective services provided by community organizations, child welfare agencies, and schools (Mental Health America, 2015).

The services need to be strength-based, recovery-oriented, family-focused, trauma-informed, individualized, and suitable for the child's gender, age, culture, and language. The main thrust of diversion is that youths should be positively engaged and also integrated in their communities and families. Generally, when it comes to diversion, the youths require the following:

- The youths need the chance to foster and nurture connections
- They need the opportunity to explore, discuss, and also reflect on their ideas

- Youths require the opportunity to create lasting impact in their community

- They need the chance to embrace creativity

- Youths require the chance to be mentored on how to make good life decisions

- They need the opportunity to have emotional safety (Mental Health America, 2015)

THE BLUEPRINT FOR CHANGE

The following key principles actually form the basis for the National Center for Mental Health and Juvenile Justice (NCMHJJ) blueprint for change (A comprehensive Model for the Identification and Treatment of Youth with Mental Health Needs in Contact with the Juvenile Justice System:

- Youth should not have to enter the juvenile justice system in order to have access to mental health services.

- When possible, juveniles with mental health conditions should be diverted to evidence-based mental health treatment in community settings.

- The information that is collected to help provide mental health screenings should not be used to jeopardize the legal interests of children as defendants.

- In the event that it is impossible to divert youth out of the justice system, they should be placed in the least restrictive environment that also has access to evidence-based treatment.

- The mental health services should be consistent with the developmental realities of youth.

- The mental health services that are provided for children should respond to issues such as ethnicity, gender, sexual orientation, race, socio-economic status, age, and religion.

- There must be a regular evaluation of the services and strategies for serving children in the juvenile justice system in order to determine their effectiveness.

- Planning and services for children has to be based on close collaboration among education, juvenile justice, and other systems.

- Mental health services need to be consistent with the developmental realities of children (Skowyra et al., 2007).

Juvenile Competency

The mental health assessment of youth offenders assists in determining how the system can help to address their treatment needs. It also helps to address the legal issues regarding a juvenile's competency to understand the adjudicatory process, and participate in it thoughtfully, and make decisions as part of the process. Ideally, incompetence to stand trial has to do with a mental disorder or developmental disability. Juvenile competency is greatly complicated by developmental immaturity with limited guidance in law regarding how to deal with it. Developmental immaturity is a factor that distinguishes many juveniles from adults in crucial ways that make them less qualified to assist in their defense or even make important decisions as part of the process. Generally, juveniles have the rights afforded to adult defendants, which includes the right to be competent to stand trial and a right to counsel (Hammond, 2007).

Conclusion

Each year, an estimated 2 million youths under the age of 18 are arrested in the United States, which translates to about 5,000 delinquency cases each day. Although, approximately 95 percent of those arrested are not accused of non-violent crimes such as rape, murder, and aggravated assault, they are still incarcerated in the juvenile justice system. This leads to more harm to the social, academic, and personal growth of the youth despite the efforts made to reduce incarceration. A large number of youths in the juvenile justice system have diagnosable mental health disorder, and approximately 75 percent of youth in the juvenile justice system have also experienced traumatic victimization like domestic abuse, physical abuse, and traumatic neglect that made them vulnerable to health disorders and PTSD (Fisher, 2015). Correctional facilities have a duty to provide adequate medical services, which includes treatment services for mental health and substance use and they are to ensure the protection of youths from harm.

Conclusion

Every child has a right to a life that is free from violence. Whenever a child is abused and neglected, we infringe upon that right. Child maltreatment and abuse affect children differently, and despite the fact that children exposed to abuse suffer severe and long-lasting negative effects, some children also go on to have lead healthy and productive lives as adults. The effect of child neglect and abuse is usually discussed in terms of behavioral, physical, societal, and psychological consequences. However, in reality, it's really difficult to separate the types of impacts. For instance, physical consequences like the damage to a child's developing brain can result in psychological implications, like emotional difficulties and cognitive delays. Also, psychological problems often lead to high-risk behaviors. For example, depression and anxiety may cause someone to likely abuse drugs or alcohol, smoke, or overeat. Also, high-risk behaviors can result in long-term physical health problems, such as cancer, obesity, and sexually transmitted diseases (Child Welfare Information Gateway, 2013).

Consistent love and care for a child will greatly enhance the developmental journey of the child. Parents who have a better understanding of parenting with much enthusiasm will nurture the child to acquire skills that maximize life potentials. However, poor parental care negatively impacts the rapid growth and changes that usually take place in the developing child from infancy to adulthood, with long-term consequences (Swain, B).

According to the National Institute of Justice, maltreated children were 11 times more likely to be arrested by law enforcement agents than a control group, and they're 2.7 times more likely to be arrested when they become adults (English et al., 2004). Abused or neglected children are more likely to become delinquent at a younger age, and they have a higher tendency to commit violent offenses (Lemmon, 1999; Ryan et al., 2007; English, 1998; English et al., 2002; Kelley et al., 1997; Widom, 1996; Widom & Maxfield, 2001). Parents should, therefore, establish a balance between home and childcare settings, and they should continue to provide a variety of intimate interactions not available in childcare centers (Ahnert et al., 2003; NICHD, 1999). According to the results of studies carried out, it has been suggested that there is a link between the quality of parent-child attachment and the outcomes much later in life, such as the level of social skill, self-esteem, and the level of aggressive behavior. A secure bond with parents helps the child develop a positive self-image and enables the child to learn to trust the parents. This may transfer to a general perception of other people as safe and reliable. Parents create a base when they are available, responsive, and a reliable source of safety and comfort to the child, and it serves as a good foundation for general interpersonal skills. The way children interact with their parents is very important, and a child's temperament might really influence the way the parents treat the child (Fitton et al.).

One of the most common reasons for the referral of children and adults to child and adolescent mental health services in Western countries is as a result of conduct disorders. Also, a great number of children and adults who have conduct disorder problems grow up to become antisocial adults with impoverished and destructive lifestyles. It's obvious that there is an increase in the case of conduct disorder in childhood in Western countries, which is placing a great personal and economic burden on both the people and the society. The effect of conduct disorder is not limited to health care services and social care agencies; it also affects other sectors, like the family, school, and criminal justice agencies (The British Psychological Society, 2013).

In addition, it is estimated that between 4 and 6 million children in America have been identified with antisocial behavior problems, and several factors could contribute to the antisocial behavior of children, such as marital discord, health issues, harsh or inconsistent disciplinary practices and learning or cognitive disabilities. To prevent antisocial behavior in children, parents should ensure a safe and secure family and social environment for their children, and they should be role models for prosocial behaviors and ensure early intervention as soon as the problem is identified (Gale Encyclopedia of Children's Health, 2017).

Also, when the opportunities to commit crime are reduced, it will go a long way toward reducing crime in the society. The University of Washington researchers evaluated 20 parenting programs and discovered five programs extremely effective in helping parents and children at all risk levels, to avoid the issue of adolescent behavior problems that affect both the individuals and the entire community. According to the assistant director of the University of Washington Social Development Research Group in the School of Social Work, Kevin Haggerty, these programs have significantly reduced depression and anxiety, reduced aggression, decreased drug use, and enhanced better mental health. Take a look at the five programs:

- Positive Parenting Program - This is a flexible system of programs that emphasize five main   goals:
- Creating positive learning environment
- Self-care for parents
- Making use of effective discipline
- Promoting safe and engaging environments
- Creating clear and reasonable expectations
- Staying Connected With Your Teen - This program helps children 12-17 years old avoid risky sexual activity, violent behavior and drug use. It was developed by Richard F. Catalano and J. David Hawkins in the University of Washington Social Work.
- Nurse-Family Partnership - Assists single mothers by sending nurses to visit young and first-time mothers who are single at least once every two weeks during their pregnancy until the child is two years old. The nurses assist expecting mothers reduce drinking, smoking and drug abuse. They also support

the mothers after the child is born by creating safe environments for the children and help develop strategies to help them deal with challenging behaviors.

- Strengthening Families Program: For Parents and Youth 10-14 - The program helps parents learn about the risk factors for parent-child bonding, substance abuse, and the effects of not adhering to parental guidelines. It also teaches parents how to manage anger and family conflict.

- The Incredible Years Program - Educates parents, teachers, and children 3-6 years on skills and strategies that will help them handle difficult situations. While the parents practice in group sessions, the children engage in therapist-led group sessions that help them develop skills such as making friends, problem-solving, and cooperating with others (Armstrong, 2013).

There is no doubt crime has a substantial impact on both the individual and society. For example, the cost to the society includes social service expenditures, criminal justice and the lost tax from incarcerated offenders. Considering the costs and consequences of crime and incarceration, it is imperative to enforce effective crime prevention and intervention strategies that will benefit both the individual and society. Despite the awareness of the need for the reduction of crime, the variability of people who engage in criminal activities greatly hinders the development of effective prevention programs. However, the identification of the predictors of crime will greatly help in developing effective preventive interventions (Suh-Ruu et al., 2010).

> *"Train up a child in the way he should go, and when he is old, he will not depart from it."*
>
> *-Proverbs 22:6 NKJV*

References

Abram, K. M., Teplin, L. A, McClelland, G. M., and Dulcan, M. K. (2003). Comorbid Psychiatric Disorders in Youth in Juvenile Detention. Archives of General Psychiatry. 2003; 60:1097–1108.

Acs, G., Loprest, P J., and Nichols, A. (2009). "Risk and Recovery: Documenting the Changing Risks to Family Incomes." Washington, DC: The Urban Institute

Agnew, R. (1990). The origins of delinquent events: an examination of offender accounts. Journal of Research in Crime and Delinquency, 1990, 27:267–294.

Ahnert, L., Lamb, M.E. (2003). Shared care: Establishing a balance between home and child care settings. Child Development 2003; 74(4):1044-1049.

Ahnert, L., Gunnar, M., Lamb, M.E., and Barthel, M. (2004). Transition to child care: Associations of infant-mother attachment, infant negative emotion, and cortisol elevations. Child Development 2004; 75(2):639–650.

Ajinkya, J. (2012). The Top 5 Facts About Women in Our Criminal Justice System. Center for American Progress.

Alexander, P. (1993). The differential effects of abuse characteristics and attachment in the prediction of long-term effects of sexual abuse. J Interpers Violence.1993; 8:346– 362

Allan, E., & Steffensmeier, D. (1989). Youth, underemployment, and property crime: differential effects of job availability and job quality on juvenile and young adult arrest rates. American Sociological Review, 54, 107–123.

Amato, P R. (2000). "The Consequences of Divorce for Adults and Children." Journal of Marriage and the Family 62(4): 1269–87.

American College of Pediatricians, (2007). Discipline of the Child. Corporal Punishment: A Scientific Review of its Use in Discipline.

American Psychiatric Association. Diagnostic and Statistical Manual of Mental Disorders: Text Revision (DSM-IV-TR). Washington, DC: American Psychiatric Association; 2000.

American Psychiatric Association. Diagnostic and Statistical Manual of Mental Disorders. 4th ed, Text Revision. Washington, DC: American Psychiatric Association Press; 2000: xxxvii, 943

American Psychological Association's Commission on: Violence and Youth (APA). (1993). Psychology's response (Vol. 1) [Summary Report]. Washington, DC.

Andre, G., Pease, K., Kendall, K., and Boulton, A. (1994). Health and Offence Histories of Young Offenders in Saskatoon, Canada. Criminal Behaviour and Mental Health. 1994; 4:163–180.

Andrews D, Bonta J. (1998). The psychology of criminal conduct. 2. Cincinnati, OH: Anderson.

Anthony, M. Social Development in 0-2-Year-Olds.

"Antisocial Behavior." Gale Encyclopedia of Children's Health: Infancy through Adolescence. Retrieved May 17, 2017 from Encyclopedia. com:

Antisocial Behavior - Causes and characteristics, Treatment. Net Industries.

Aos, S., Miller, M., & Drake, E. (2006). Evidence-Based Public Policy Options to Reduce Future Prison Construction, Criminal Justice Costs, and Crime Rates. Olympia, Wash.: Washington State Institute for Public Policy

Armstrong, D. (2013) 5 effective parenting programs to reduce problem behaviors in children. University of Washington Today. Retrieved from

Atkins, L., Pumariega, A., Rogers, K., Montgomery, L., Nybro, C., Jeffers, G., and Sease F. (1999). Mental health and incarcerated youth—I: Prevalence and nature of psychopathology. J. Child. Fam. Stud. 1999;8:193–204. doi: 10.1023/A:1022040018365.

Austin, R.L. (1978). Race, father-absence, and female delinquency. Criminology 15:487-504.

Baglivio, M. T., Epps, N., Swartz, K., Sayedul Huq, M., Sheer, A., & Hardt, N. S. (2014). The prevalence of adverse childhood experiences (ACE) in the lives of juvenile offenders. Journal of Juvenile Justice, 3(2).

Bauermeister, J. A., Pingel, E. S., Jadwin-Cakmak, L., Harper, G. W., Horvath, K., Weiss, G., and Dittus, P. (2015). Acceptability and Preliminary Efficacy of a Tailored Online HIV/STI Testing Intervention for Young Men who have Sex with Men: The Get Connected! Program. AIDS Behav. 2015 Oct; 19(10): 1860–1874.

Bauman, L.J., & Friedman, S.B. (1998). Corporal punishment. Pediatric Clinics of North America. 1998.45; 2; 403-414.

Baumrind, D. (1973). The development of instrumental competence through socialization. Minnesota Symp Child Psych. 1973; 7: 3-46.

Beeghley, M.E., Cicchetti., D.A. (1996). Child maltreatment, attachment, and the self-system: emergence of an internal state lexicon in toddlers at high social risk. In: Hertzig M, Farber E, eds. Annual Progress in Child Psychiatry and Child Development. Philadelphia, PA: Brunner/Mazel; 1996:127–166

Behrman, R.E., and Kliegman, R.M. (2002). Textbook of Pediatrics, Fourteenth Edition. 2002; pp 45-50. WB Saunders Company.

Belsky, J., Vandell, D. L., Burchinal, M., Clarke-Stewart, K. A., McCartney, K., & Owen, M. T. (2007). Are There Long-Term Effects of Early Child Care? Child Development, 78(2), 681-701. doi: 10.1111/j.1467-8624.2007.01021.x

Benard, B. (1995). Fostering resilience in children. (ERIC Document Reproduction Service No. ED 386 327).

Best Practices to Prevent Youth Violence. (2003). Minnesota Department of Health.

Björkqvist, K., and Niemelä, P. (1992). "New Trends in the Study of Female Aggression," in Of Mice and Women: Aspects of Female Aggression, edited by Kaj Björkqvist and Pirkko Niemelä (San Diego: Academic Press, 1992), pp.

Bock, G. R., and Goode, J. A. (2007). Introduction: Concepts of Antisocial Behavior, of Cause, and of Genetic Influences. DOI: 10.1002/9780470514825.ch1

Bock, G.R., and J.A. Goode, ed. (1996). Genetics of Criminal and Antisocial Behavior. Toronto: Wiley & Sons.

Bouris, A., Guilamo-Ramos, V., Pickard, A., Shiu, C., Loosier, P. S., Dittus, P., Gloppen, K., and Waldmiller, J. M. A systematic review of parental influences on the health and well-being of lesbian, gay, and bisexual youth: time for new public health research and practice agenda. Journal of Primary Prevention 2010; 3:273–309

Bouris, A., and Everett, B. G., Heath, R. D., Elsaesser, C. E., Neilands, T.B. (2016) Effects of Victimization and Violence on Suicidal Ideation and Behaviors Among Sexual Minority and Heterosexual Adolescents. LGBT Health 2016; 3(2): 153-61.

Braverman, J. (2013). The Human Life Cycle Stages, Livestrong.com.

Bremner, J.D., Vythilingham, M., Vermetten, E., et al. (2003). Cortisol response to a cognitive stress challenge in posttraumatic stress disorder (PTSD) related to childhood abuse. Psychoneuroendocrinology.2003; 28 (6):733– 750

Brennan, P., Mednick, S., & John, R. (1989). Specialization in violence: evidence of a criminal subgroup. Criminology, 1989, 27:437–453

Briggs, C.M., and Cutright, P. (1994). Structural and cultural determinants of child homicide: a cross-national analysis. Violence and Victims, 1994, 9:3–16.

Broidy, L. M., Nagin, D. S., Tremblay, R. E., Bates, J. E., Brame, B., Dodge, K. A.,... Vitaro, F. (2003). "Developmental Trajectories of Childhood Disruptive Behaviors and Adolescent Delinquency: A Six-Site, Cross-National Study," Developmental Psychology. Special Issue: Violent Children 39, no. 2 (2003): 222–45.

Bronfenbrenner, U., and Ceci, S. J. (1994). Nature-nurture recon-ceptualization in developmental perspective: A bioecological model, Psychological Review, 101, 568-586.

Brooks, R. B. (1994). Children at Risk: Fostering resiliency and hope. American Journal of Orthopsychiatry, 64, 545-553.

Brown, M. (2006). "Gender, Ethnicity, and Offending over the Life Course: Women's Pathways to Prison in the Aloha State," Critical Criminology 14, no. 2 (2006): 137–58

Brunner, H.G., Nelen, M., Breakefield, X. O., Ropers, H. H., and Van Ost, B.A. (1993). Abnormal Behavior Associated with a Point Mutation in the Structural Gene for Monoamine Oxidase A.

Bureau of Justice Statistics. http://www.bjs.gov

Bureau of Justice Statistics. (2005). www.ojp.usdoj.gov/bjs. Accessed on May 1, 2008.

Burwick, A., Oddo, V., Durso, L., Friend, D., and Gates, G. (2014). Identifying and Serving LGBTQ Youth: Case Studies of Runaway and Homeless Youth Program Grantees. Washington, D.C.: U.S.

Butts, J.A., Bazemore, G., and Meroe, A.S. (2010). Positive Youth Justice-Framing Justice Interventions.

Buvinic, M., Morrison, A., & Shifter, M. (1999). Violence in Latin America and the Caribbean: a framework for action. Washington, DC, Inter-American Development Bank, 1999.

Campaniello, N. (2014). Women in crime. IZA World of Labor 2014: 105 doi: 10.15185/izawol.105 Nadia Campaniello © November 2014 wol.iza.org

Campbell, S. B. (1995). Behaviour problems in preschool children: A review of recent research, Journal of Child Psychology and Psychiatry, 36, 1, 115-119.

Cantor, D., & Land, K. C. (1985). Unemployment and crime rates in the post-World War II United States: a theoretical and empirical analysis. American Sociological Review, 53, 317–322.

Capaldi, D. M., Kim, H. K., and Shortt, J. W. (2004). "Women's Involvement in Aggression in Young Adult Romantic Relationships: A Developmental Systems Model," in Aggression, Antisocial Behavior, and Violence among Girls: A Developmental Perspective, Duke Series in Child Development and Public Policy, edited by Martha Putallaz and Karen Bierman (New York: Guilford Publications, 2004), pp. 223–41.

Capaldi, D.M., and Patterson, G.R. (1996). Can violent offenders be distinguished from frequent offenders? Prediction from childhood to adolescence. Journal of Research in Crime and Delinquency 33:206-231.

Cavanagh, S E., and Huston, C A. (2008). "The Timing of Family Instability and Children's Social Development." Journal of Marriage and Family 70:1258–69.

Centers for Disease Control and Prevention (CDC). (2017). Youth Violence: Prevention Strategies.

Centers for Disease Control and Prevention (CDC). Lesbian, Gay, Bisexual, and Transgender Health: LGBT Youth. Retrieved from https://www.cdc.gov/lgbthealth/youth.htm

Centers for Disease Control and Prevention. HIV Surveillance Report, (2014); vol. 26. Published November 2015. Accessed October 2016.

Center for Effective Collaboration and Practice. (2001, September). Early warning, timely response: A guide to safe schools. Selected Resources Reviewed.

Center for the Study of Social Policy & Administration on Children , Youth and Families. (2013). CONNECTING THE DOTS: CSSP's Str engthening Families and Youth Thrive Frameworks & ACYF's Litera ture Review on Protective Factors for In Risk Children. Washington, DC.

Center for the Study of Social Policy. (n.d.). Social connec- tions. Washington, DC: Author. http://www.cssp.org/reform/child- welfare/youth-thrive/2013/YT_Social-Connections.pdf

Center for the Study of Social Policy. (n.d.). Youth resil- ience. Washington, DC: Author. http://www.cssp.org/reform/child- welfare/youth-thrive/2013/YT_Youth-Resilience.pdf

Child Welfare Information Gateway. (2013). Long-term Consequences of Child Abuse and Neglect.

Chiodo, D., Leschied, P.C., Whitehead, P.C., & Hurley, D. (2008). Child welfare practice and policy related to the impact of children experiencing physical victimization and domestic violence Children and Youth Services Review, 30(5), 564–574

Clarke, J.W. (1998). The Lineaments of Wrath: Race, Violent Crime, and American Culture. Somerset, NJ: Transaction Publishers.

Cloward, R., & Ohlin, L. (1960). Delinquency and opportunity. New York, NY: Free Press.

Cocozza, J., and Skowyra, K. (2000). Youth with mental health disorders: Issues and emerging responses. Off. Juv. Justice Delinquency Prev. J. 2000; 7:3–13.

Cohen, L., & Felson, M. (1979). Social change and crime rates. American Sociological Review, 44, 588–608.

Coker, T. R., Austin, S. B., and Schuster, M. A. (2010). The health and health care of lesbian, gay, and bisexual adolescents. Annual Review of Public Health 2010; 31:457–477.

Connor, D. F. (2002). Aggression and Antisocial Behavior in Children and Adolescents. New York: Guilford Press, 2002.

Cook, A. (2003). Complex Trauma in Children and Adolescents. Los Angeles, CA: National Child Traumatic Stress Network; 2003.

Craigie, T L., Brooks-Gunn, J., and Waldfogel, J. (2012). "Family Structure, Family Stability and Outcomes of Five-Year-Old Children." Families, Relationships, and Societies 1(1): 43–61.

Crisp, T. Dreams, Health, yoga, mind & spirit.

Crutchfield, R. D., & Pitchford, S. (1997). Work and crime: the effects of labor stratification. Social Forces, 76 (1), 93–118.

Cummings, E., & Davies, P. (2002). Effects of marital conflict on children: recent advance and emerging themes in process-oriented research. Journal of Child Psychology and Psychiatry. 2002; 43: 31-63.

Curran, D. J. and Renzetti, C. M. (2001). Theories of Crime, Boston: Allyn and Bacon. DALY, K. (1988). 'Rethinking Judicial Paternalism: Gender, Work-Family Relations, and Sentencing', Gender and Society, 3(1): 9–36. Freud, Sigmund. (1933). New Introductory Lectures

Dahlberg, L.L., and Potter, L.B. (2001). Youth violence: developmental pathways and prevention challenges. American Journal of Preventive Medicine, 2001, 20(1S):3–14.

Daniel, B., Wassell, S., & Gilligan, R. (2010). Child Development for Child Care and Protection Workers (2nd ed). Jessica Kingsley Publishers: London, United Kingdom.

Davis, N. J. (1999). Resilience: Status of the research and research-based programs. Retrieved July 21, 2001, from Substance Abuse and Mental Health Services Administration, Center for Mental Health Services, Division of Program Development, Special Populations & Projects, Special Programs Development Branch

Deater-Deckard, K., Dodge, K.A., Bates, J.E., & Pettit, G.S. (1996). Physical discipline among African American and European American mothers: Links to children's externalizing behaviors. Developmental Psychology. 1996; 32:1065-1072.

De Bellis, M.D., Keshavan, M.S., Clark, D.B., et al. Developmental traumatology, part II: brain development. Biol Psychiatry.1999;45 (10):1271– 1284

DeBord, K. Learning in Families Together: "School-Agers" 5 to 8 Years. Virginia Cooperative Extension, Virginia Tech. Virginia State University. Publication FCS-63P

Department of Health and Human Services, Administration for Children & Families, Office of Planning, Research, and Evaluation.

Department of Human Services. (2007). Every child every chance: Child Development and Trauma Guide. Victoria, Australia – a significant amount of information for this resource, particularly regarding the indicators of trauma, came from this document

De Pedro, K. T., Esqueda, M. C., and Gilreath, T. D. (2017). School Protective Factors and Substance Use Among Lesbian, Gay, and Bisexual Adolescents in California Public Schools. LGBT Health. 2017 Jun; 4(3):210-216. Doi: 10.1089/lgbt.2016.0132. Epub 2017 May 12.

Derzon, J.H., and Lipsey, M.W. (2000). The correspondence of family features with problem, aggressive, criminal and violent behavior. Unpublished manuscript. Nashville, TN: Institute for Public Policy Studies, Vanderbilt University.

Devine, P., Coolbaugh, K., and Jenkins, S. (1998). Disproportionate minority confinement: Lessons learned from five states. Juvenile Justice Bulletin, December, Office of Juvenile Justice and Delinquency Prevention. Washington, DC: U.S. Department of Justice.

Dietz, T.L. (2000). Disciplining Children: Characteristics Associated With the Use of Corporal Punishment. Child Abuse & Neglect. 2000; (24)12:1529-1542.

Dishion, T. A., French, D. C., & Patterson, G. R. (1995). The development and ecology of antisocial behavior. In D. Cicchetti & D. J. Cohe (Eds.), Developmental psychopathology: Risk, disorder, and adaptation (Vol. 2, pp. 421-471). New York: John Wiley.

Dobbin, S. A., & Gatowski, S. I. (1996). Juvenile Violence: A Guide to Research. Reno, NV: National Council of Juvenile and Family Court Judges.

Dodge, K. A., Bates, J. E. & Pettit, G. S. (1990). Mechanisms in the cycle of violence, Science 250:1678-1683

Eamon, M.K. (2002). Poverty, parenting, peer, and neighborhood influences on young adolescent antisocial behavior. J Soc Serv Res. 2002; 28:1-23.

Ehrlich, I. (1973). Participation in illegitimate activities: a theoretical and empirical investigation. Journal of Political Economy, 81 (3), 521–565.

Elizabeth, C. (2008). Understanding the Female Offender.

Elliott, D.S. (1994). Longitudinal research in criminology: Promise and practice. Pp. 189-201 in Cross National Longitudinal Research on Human Development and Criminal Behavior, E.G.M. Weitekamp and H.-J. Kerner, eds. Boston: Kluwer Academic Publishers.

Elliott, D.S. (1994b). Serious violent offenders: Onset, developmental course, and termination. Criminology 32(1):1-21.

Elliott, D.S., Huizinga, D., and Ageton, S.S. (1985). Explaining Delinquency and Drug Use. Beverly Hills, CA: Sage.

Elliott, D.S., and Menard, S. (1996). Delinquent friends and delinquent behavior. Delinquency and Crime, J.D. Hawkins, ed. New York: Cambridge University Press.

Elzinga, B.M., Schmal, C.G., Vermetten, E., van Dyck, R., and Bremner, J.D. (2003). Higher cortisol levels following exposure to traumatic reminders in abuse-related PTSD. Neuropsychopharmacology.2003; 28 (9):1656– 1665

English, D.J. (1998). The extent and consequences of child maltreatment The Future of Children: Protecting Children from Abuse and Neglect, 8(1), 39–53

English, D.J., Widom, C.S., & Brandford, C. (2002). Childhood victimization and delinquency, adult criminality, and violent criminal behavior: A replication and extension. Final report presented to the National Institute of Justice, grant 97-IJCX-0017

English, D.J., Widom, C.S., & Brandford, C. (2004). Another look at the effects of child abuse NIJ Journal, 25, 23–24

Espelage, D. L., Aragon, S. R., and Birkett, M. (2008). Homophobic teasing, psychological outcomes, and sexual orientation among high school students: What influence do parents and schools have? School Psychology Review 2008; 37:202–216

Eth S, ed. PTSD in children and adolescents. In: Oldham JM, Riba MB, series eds. Review of Psychiatry. Series Vol 20. Washington, DC: American Psychiatric Association Press; 2001:1– 200

Evans, G W., Brooks-Gunn, J., and Klebanov, P K. (2011). "Stressing Out the Poor: Chronic Physiological Stress and the Income-Achievement Gap." Community Investments 23(2): 22–27.

Evans, G W., and Schamberg, M A. (2009). "Childhood Poverty, Chronic Stress, and Adult Working Memory." Proceedings of the National Academy of Sciences 106(16): 6545–49.

Fagan, A. (2005). The relationship between adolescent physical abuse and criminal offending: Support for an enduring and generalized cycle of violence Journal of Family Violence, 20(5), 279–290

Fagan, J., and Browne, A. (1994). Violence between spouses and intimates: physical aggression between women and men in intimate relationships. In: Reiss AJ, Roth JA, eds. Understanding and preventing violence: panel on the understanding and control of violent behavior. Vol. 3. Social influences. Washington, DC, National Academy Press, 1994:114–292.

Farrington, D.P. (1986). "Age and Crime," in Crime and Justice: An Annual Review of Research, vol. 7, eds. Michael Tonry and Norval Morris, Chicago, Ill.: University of Chicago Press, 1986: 189-250.

Farrington, D.P. (1986a). Age and crime. Crime and Justice: An Annual Review of Research 7:29-90.

Farrington, D.P. (1983). Offending from 10 to 25 years of age. Pp. 17-37 in Prospective Studies of Crime and Delinquency, K.T. VanDusen and S.A. Mednick, eds. Boston: Kluwer-Nijhoff.

Farrington, D.P. (1989). Early predictors of adolescent aggression and adult violence. Violence and Victims 4:79-100.

Farrington, D.P., and R. Loeber. (1999). Transatlantic replicability of risk factors in the development of delinquency. Pp. 299-329 in Historical and Geographical Influences on Psychopathology, P. Cohen, C. Slomkowski, and L.N. Robins, eds. Mahwah, NJ: Lawrence Erlbaum Associates.

Farrington, D.P. (2001). Predicting adult official and self-reported violence. In: Pinard GF, Pagani L, eds. Clinical assessment of dangerousness: empirical contributions. Cambridge, Cambridge University Press, 2001:66–88.

Farrington, D.P. (1993). Motivations for conduct disorder and delinquency. Development and Psychopathology, 1993, 5:225–241.

Felitti, V.J., Anda, R.F., Nordenberg P, et al. (1998). Relationship of childhood abuse and household dysfunction to many of the leading causes of death in adults. The Adverse Childhood Experiences (ACE) Study. Am J Prev Med.1998; 14 (4):245– 258

Fergusson, D. M., Horwood, L. J., and Ridder, E. M. (2005). Show me a child at seven: consequences of conduct problems in childhood for psychosocial functioning in adulthood. Journal of Child Psychology and Psychiatry. 2005; 46:837–49. [PubMed]

Fitton, V., and Koehler, R. Parent-Child Attachment Relationships and the Effects of Attachment Disruption. Michigan State University School of Social Work.

Finley, M. (1994). Cultivating resilience: An overview for rural educators and parents. (ERIC Document Reproduction Service No. ED 372 904)

Fisher, N. (2015) 4 Things To Understand About Youth, Mental Health & Juvenile Justice In The US.

Fonagy, P. (2001). The human genome and the representational world: The role of early mother-infant interaction in creating an inter-personal interpretive mechanism. Bulletin of the Menninger Clinic. 65, 427-447.

Fried C., and Reppucci, D. (2001). Criminal decision making: The development of adolescent judgment, criminal responsi-bility and culpability. Law Hum. Behav. 2001; 25:45–61. doi: 10.1023/A:1005639909226.

Friedman, M. S., Marshal, M. P., Guadamuz, T. E., Wei, C., Wong, C. F., Saewyc, E. M., and Stall, R. (2011). "A Meta-Analysis of Disparities in Childhood Sexual Abuse, Parental Physical Abuse, and Peer Victimization Among Sexual Minority and Sexual Nonminority Individuals." American Journal of Public Health 101(8):1481–94.

Gale Encyclopedia of Children's Health: Infancy through Adolescence. "Antisocial Behavior." Retrieved May 17, 2017 from Encyclopedia. com:

Garascia, J. A. (2005). The price we are willing to pay for punitive justice in the juvenile justice system: Mentally ill delinquents and their disproportionate share of the burden. Indiana Law J. 2005;80:489–515.

Garmezy, N. (1993). Children in Poverty: Resilience despite risk. Psychiatry, 56, 127-136.

Garnette, L., Irvine, A., Reyes, C., and Wilber, S. (2011). Lesbian, Gay, Bisexual, and Transgender (LGBT) Youth and the Juvenile Justice System, in Juvenile Justice: Advancing Research, Policy, and Practice (eds F. T. Sherman and F. H. Jacobs), John Wiley & Sons, Inc., Hoboken, New Jersey. Doi: 10.1002/9781118093375.ch8

Gartner, R. (1990). The victims of homicide: a temporal and cross-national comparison. American Sociological Review, 1990, 55:92–106.

George, C., & Main, M. (1979). Social interactions of young abused children: approach, avoidance and aggression, Child Development, 50, 306-318.

Giordano, P. C., Stephen, A., Cernkovich., and Lowery, A. R. (2004). "A Long-Term Follow-Up of Serious Adolescent Female Offenders," in Aggression, Antisocial Behavior, and Violence among Girls: A Developmental Perspective, Duke Series in Child Development and Public Policy, edited by Martha Putallaz and Karen Bierman (New York: Guilford Publications, 2004), pp. 186–202.

Glaze, L. E. & Palla, S. (2005). Probation and parole in the United States, 2004, Bureau of Justice Statistics.

Goldstein, H. (1977). Policing of a free society. Cambridge, MA, Ballinger, 1977.

Goodenow, C., Szalacha, L., and Westheimer, K. (2006). School support groups, other school factors, and the safety of sexual minority adolescents. Psychology in the Schools 2006; 43:573–89.

Gorner, J. (2016) Chicago Tops 700 Homicide – with a Month to go in violent 2016, Chicago Tribune December 2, 2016.

Gottfredson, G.D., and Gottfredson, D.C. (1985). Victimization in Schools. New York, NY: Plenum Press.

Greenberg, D. F. (1985). Age, crime, and social explanation. American Journal of Sociology, 91, 1–21.

Griffin, P. (2007). National overviews. In State Juvenile Justice Profiles. Pittsburgh, PA: National Center for Juvenile Justice. www.ncjj.org/stateprofiles/

Grisso, T. (2008). Adolescent offenders with mental disorders. Future Child. 2008; 18:143–164. doi: 10.1353/foc.0.0016

Grotberg, E. H. (1995). A Guide to Promoting Resilience in Children: Strengthening the Human Spirit. Retrieved April 11, 2001, from The International Resilience Project from the Early Childhood Development: Practice and Reflections Series, Bernard Van Leer Foundation

Haller, M.H. (1989) Bootlegging: The business and politics of violence. Pp. 146-162 in Violence in America, Volume 1: The History of Crime, T.R. Gurr, ed. Newbury Park, CA: Sage.

Haskins, R., and Barnett, W.S. (Eds.) 2011. Investing in Young Children: New Directions in Federal Preschool and Early Childhood Policy. (Brookings Center on Children and Families & National Institute for Early Education Research, New Brunswick, 2010); http://nieer.org/pdf/Investing_in_Young_Children.pdf. Accessed 6 June 2014.

Hammond, S. (2007). Mental Health Needs of Juvenile Offenders. National Conference of State Legislatures ISBN 1-58024-XXX-X

Harold, G., Kerr, D., van Ryzin, M., DeGarmo, D., Rhoades, K., and Leve L. (2013). Depressive symptom trajectories among girls in the juvenile justice system: 24-Month Outcomes of an RCT of Multidimensional Treatment Foster Care. Pre. Sci. 2013;14:437–446. doi: 10.1007/s11121-012-0317-y.

Hatzenbuehler ML, Birkett M, Van Wagenen A, Meyer IH. Protective school climates and reduced risk for suicide ideation in sexual minority youth. Am J Pub Health. 2014; 104(2):279-286.

Hatzenbuehler ML, Keyes KM. Inclusive anti-bullying policies reduce suicide attempts in lesbian and gay youth. J Adolesc Health. 2013; 53(1 Suppl): S21—S26.

Hawkins, J.D., Battin, S.R., K.G. Hill, R.D. Abbott., and Catalano, R.F. (1998). The contribution of gang membership to delinquency beyond delinquent friends. Criminology 36(1):93-115.

Hawkins, J.D., Arthur, M.W., and Catalano, R.F. (1995b). Preventing substance abuse. Pp. 343-427 in Building a Safer Society: Strategic Approaches to Crime Prevention: Volume 19, Crime and Justice: A Review of the Research, M. Tonry and D.P. Farrington, eds. Chicago: University of Chicago Press.

Heck, N. C., Livingston, N. A., Flentje, A., Oost, K., Stewart, B. T., and Cochran, B. N. (2014). "Reducing Risk for Illicit Drug Use and Prescription Drug Misuse: High School Gay–Straight Alliances and Lesbian, Gay, Bisexual, and Transgender Youth." Addictive Behaviors 39:824–28.

Heal, K. (1978). Misbehavior among school children: The roles of the school in strategies for prevention. Policy and Politics 6:321–332.

Heck, N. C., Livingston, N. A., Flentje, A., Oost, K., Stewart, B. T., and Cochran, B. N. (2014). Reducing risk for illicit drug use and prescription drug misuse: High school gay-straight alliances and lesbian, gay, bisexual, and transgender youth. Addictive Behaviors. 2014; 39:824-828.

Heide, K. M. (2003). "Youth Homicide: A Review of the Literature and a Blueprint for Action," International Journal of Offender Therapy and Comparative Criminology 47, no.1 (2003): 6–36;

Heilbrun, K., Lee, R., and Cottle, C. (2005).Risk Factors and Intervention Outcomes: Meta-Analyses of Juvenile Offending. In: Heilbrun K., Goldstein N., Redding R., editors. Juvenile Delinquency: Prevention, Assessment, and Treatment. Oxford University Press; Oxford, UK: 2005.

Herrenkohl, T.I., Hawkins, J.D., Chung, I.J., Hill, K.G., and Battin-Pearson, S. (2001). School and community risk factors and interventions. In Child Delinquents: Development, Intervention, and Service Needs, edited by R. Loeber and D.P. Farrington. Thousand Oaks, CA: Sage Publications, Inc., pp. 211–246.

Hickey, J. G. (2016). Chicago's grim murder trend blamed on light sentencing, misguided reforms. Fox News U.S

Holbrook, T.L., Hoyt, D.B., Coimbra, R., Potenza, B., Sise, M., and Anderson, J.P. (2005). Long-term trauma persists after major trauma in adolescents: new data on risk factors and functional outcome. J Trauma.2005; 58 (4):764– 771

Holman, B., and Ziedenberg, J. (2006). The Dangers of Detention: The Impact of Incarcerating Youth in Detention and Other Secure Facilities. Washington, DC. Justice Policy Institute. P. 2.

Home Office Statistical Bulletin. (1995). Criminal Careers of Those Born between 1953 and 1973 (London: Home Office, 1995).

Huebner, D. M., and Thoma, B. C. (2015). Neilands TB. School victimization and substance use among lesbian, gay, bisexual, and transgender adolescents. Prev Sci 2015; 16(5): 734-43.

Huh, D., Tristan, J., and Wade, E. (2006). "Does Problem Behavior Elicit Poor Parenting? A Prospective Study of Adolescent Girls," Journal of Adolescent Research 21, no. 2 (2006): 185–204.

Human Rights Campaign. Teen Dating Violence Among LGBTQ Youth. Filed under: Children & Youth, Transgender, Transgender Children & Youth. Retrieved from http://www.hrc.org/resources/teen-dating-violence-among-lgbtq-youth

Hunt, J., and Moodie-Mills, A. C. (2012). The Unfair Criminalization of Gay and Transgender Youth: An Overview of the Experiences of LGBT Youth in the Juvenile Justice System. Center for American Progress

Ibid.; Giordano, P. C., and Cernkovich, S. A. (1997). "Gender and Antisocial Behavior," in Handbook of Antisocial Behavior, edited by David Stoff, James Breiling, and Jack Maser (Hoboken, N.J.: John Wiley & Sons Inc., 1997), pp. 496–510.

Institute of Medicine, Committee on Integrating the Science of Early Childhood Development. From Neurons to Neighborhoods: The Science of Early Child Development. Shonkoff J, Phillips D, eds. Washington, DC: National Academies Press; 2000

Institute of Medicine and National Research Council. (2001). Juvenile Crime, Juvenile Justice. Washington, DC: The National Academies Press. doi: 10.17226/9747.

Irvine, A. (2010). "'We've Had Three of Them: Addressing the Invisibility of Lesbian, Gay, Bisexual, and Gender Nonconforming Youths in the Juvenile Justice System." Columbia Journal of Gender and Law 19(3):675–701.

Isaacs, J B. (2013). "Unemployment from a Child's Perspective." Washington, DC: First Focus and the Urban Institute.

Islam, J., and Nurjahan, K. (2013). On the Etiology of Female Offending in Bangladesh: Toward a Quest for the Alternative Explanation, European Academic Research, Vol-1, Issue- 4 (July).

Jaffee, S. R., Belsky, J., Harrington, H., Caspi, A., and Moffitt, T. E. (2006). "When Parents Have a History of Conduct Disorder: How Is the Caregiving Environment Affected?" Journal of Abnormal Psychology 115, no. 2 (2006): 309–19

Jarquin, E., & Carrillo, F. (1997). La econo´mica poli´tica de la reforma judicial. [The political economy of judicial reform.] Washington, DC, Inter-American Development Bank, 1997.

Jones, C. M. (2005). Genetic and Environmental Influences on Criminal Behavior- Rochester Institute of Technology.

Jones, T., and McMahon. (2014). Tips for Preventing Delinquent Behavior.

Joseph, J. (2001). Is crime in the genes? A critical review of twin and adoption studies of criminality and antisocial behavior. The Journal of Mind and Behavior, 22, 179-218.

Jonson-Reid, M., & Barth, R.P. (2000). From maltreatment report to juvenile incarceration: The role of child welfare services Child Abuse & Neglect, 24, 505–520

JRank Articles- Causes of Crime: Explaining Crime, Physical Abnormalities, Psychological Disorders, Social And Economic Factors, Broken Windows, Income, And Education.

Justice and Delinquency Prevention. Washington, DC: U.S. Department of Justice.

Kalil, A., and Wightman, P. (2011). "Parental Job Loss and Children's Educational Attainment in Black and White Middle-Class Families." Social Science Quarterly 92(1): 57–78.

Kalil, A., and Ziol-Guest, K M. (2008). "Parental Employment Circumstances and Children's Academic Progress." Social Science Research 37(2): 500–15.

Kandel, E., Brennan, P.A., Mednick, S.A., and Michelson, N.M. (1989). Minor physical abnormalities and recidivistic adult violent criminal behavior. Acta Psychiatrica Scandinavia 79:103-107.

Kandel, E., and Mednick, S.A. (1991). Perinatal complications predict violent offending. Criminology 29:519-520.

Kann, L., Olsen, E. O, McManus T, et al. (2015). Sexual Identity, Sex of Sexual Contacts, and Health-Related Behaviors Among Students in Grades 9-12 – United States and Selected Sites, 2015. MMWR Surveill Summ 2016; 65(9): 1-202.

Keenan, k., and Shaw, D. S. (2003). "Starting at the Beginning: Exploring the Etiology of Antisocial Behavior in the First Years of Life," in Causes of Conduct Disorder and Juvenile Delinquency, edited by Benjamin Lahey, Terrie E. Moffitt, and Avshalom Caspi (New York: Guilford Press, 2003), pp. 153–81;

Kelley, B.T., Thornberry., T.P., & Smith, C.A. (1997). In the wake of childhood maltreatment. Washington, DC: OJJDP, Juvenile Justice Bulletin

Kopp, C.B., and J.B. Krakow. (1983). The developmentalist and the study of biological risk: A view of the past with an eye toward the future. Child Development 54:1086-1108.

Kraushaar, K., & Alsop, B. (1995). A naturalistic alcohol availability experiment: effects on crime. Washington, DC, Educational Resources Information Center, 1995 (document CG 026 940).

Lamb, M.E. (2000). The effects of quality of care on child development. Applied Developmental Science 2000; 4(3):112-115.

Landenberger, N.A., and Lipsey, M.W. (2005). "The Positive Effects of Cognitive-behavioral Programs for Offenders: A Meta-analysis of Factors Associated With Effective Treatment," Journal of Experimental Criminology, 1 (2005): 451-476.

Lane, R. (1986). Roots of Violence in Black Philadelphia 1860-1900. Cambridge, MA: Harvard University Press.

Langlois, M. Risk Factors and Intervention Strategies for Gay, Lesbian, Bisexual, and Transgender Youth, National Association of Social Workers.

Lansford, J.E., Dodge, K.A., Pettit, G.S., Bates, J.E., Crozier, J., and Kaplow, J.A. (2002). 12-year prospective study of the long-term effects of early child physical maltreatment on psychological, behavioral, and academic problems in adolescence. Arch Pediatr Adolesc Med. 2002; 156 (8):824– 830

Lareau, Annette (2011). Unequal Childhoods. University of California Press. pp. 2–4. ISBN 978-0-520-27142-5.

Laub, J.H., and Sampson, R.J. (1988). Unraveling families and delinquency: A reanalysis of the Gluecks' data. Criminology 26(3):355-380.

Laughlin, L. (2010). Who's minding the kids? Childcare Arrangements: Spring 2005/Summer 2006. Current Population Reports P70-121. Washington, DC: U.S. Census Bureau.

LeBlanc. M., and Frechette, M. (1989). Male criminal activity from childhood through youth. New York, NY, SpringerVerlag.

Lemmon, J.H. (1999). How child maltreatment affects dimensions of juvenile delinquency in a cohort of low-income urban youths Justice Quarterly, 16, 357–376

Leve, L., and Chamberlain, P. (2007). A randomized evaluation of multidimensional treatment foster care: Effects on school attendance and homework completion in juvenile justice girls. Res. Soc. Work Pract. 2007;17:657–663. doi: 10.1177/1049731506293971

Lipsey, M.W. (2009). "The Primary Factors That Characterize Effective Interventions With Juvenile Offenders: A meta-analytic overview," Victims and Offenders 4 (2009): 124-147.

Lipsey, M.W., and J.H. Derzon. (1998). Predictors of violent or serious delinquency in adolescence and early adulthood: A synthesis of longitudinal research. Pp. 86-105 in Serious and Violent Juvenile Offenders: Risk Factors and Successful Interventions, R. Loeber and D. Farrington, eds. Thousand Oaks, CA: Sage

Liska, A.E., and Reed, M.D. (1985). Ties to conventional institutions and delinquency: Estimating reciprocal effects. American Sociological Review 50(August):547-560.

Loeber, R., Farrington, D.P., and Petechuk, D. (2003). Child Delinquency: Early Intervention and Prevention. U.S. Department of Justice Child Delinquency Bulletin Series.

Loeber, R., Farrington, D. P., and Petechuk, D. (2003). Child Delinquency: Early Intervention and Prevention. U.S. Department of Justice, Office of Juvenile Justice and Delinquency Prevention.

Loeber, R., and Hay, D. (1997). "Key Issues in the Development of Aggression and Violence from Childhood to Early Adulthood," Annual Review of Psychology 48 (1997): 371–410.

Loeber, R., and Keenan, K. (1994). Interaction between conduct disorder and its comorbid conditions: Effects of age and gender. Clin. Psychol. Rev. 1994;14:497–523. doi:10.1016/0272-7358(94)90015-9

Loeber, R., and Stouthamer-Loeber, M. (1986). Family factors as correlates and predictors of juvenile conduct problems and delinquency. Pp. 29-149 in Crime and Justice, M. Tonry, N. Morris, et al., eds. Chicago: University of Chicago Press.

Lowenstein, L. F. (2003). The genetic aspects of criminality. Journal of Human Behavior in the Social Environment, 8, 63-78

Majd, K., Marksamer, J., & Reyes, C. (2009). Hidden injustice: Lesbian, gay, bisexual, and transgender youth in juvenile courts. New York, NY: The Center for HIV Law and Policy.

Marens, S., & Schaefer, M. (1988). Community policing, schools, and mental health. In: Elliott DS, Hamburg BA, Williams KR, eds. Violence in American schools. Cambridge, Cambridge University Press, 1998:312–347.

Miczek, K.A, et al. (1994). Alcohol, drugs of abuse, aggression, and violence. In: Reiss AJ, Roth JA, eds. Understanding and preventing violence: panel on the understanding and control of violent behavior. Vol. 3. Social influences. Washington, DC, National Academy Press, 1994:377–570.

Maruna, S. (2001). Making good: how ex-convicts reform and rebuild their lives. Washington, DC: American Psychological Association.

Matheny Jr, A P., Wachs, T D., Ludwig, J L., and Kay, P. (1995). "Bringing Order Out of Chaos: Psychometric Characteristics of the Confusion, Hubbub, and Order Scale." Journal of Applied Developmental Psychology 16: 429–44.

Matsueda, R., & Heimer, K. (1997). A symbolic interactionist theory of role-transitions, role-commitments, and delinquency. In T. B. Thornberry (Ed.), Developmental theories of crime and delinquency. New Brunswick, NJ: Transaction.

McCartney, K. (2004). Current Research on Child Care Effects. Retrieved August 17, 2009, at http://www.child-encyclopedia.com/Pages/PDF/McCartneyANGxp.pdf

McCord, J. (1983). A forty-year perspective on effects of child abuse and neglect. Child Abuse and Neglect 7:265-270.

McCord, J. (1979). Some child–rearing antecedents of criminal behavior in adult men. Journal of Personality and Social Psychology 37(9):1477–1486.

McCord, J. (1991). The cycle of crime and socialization practices. The Journal of Criminal Law and Criminology 82(1):211-228.

McCord, J., and Ensminger, M. (1997). Multiple risks and comorbidity in an African American population. Criminal Behavior and Mental Health 7: 339-352

McCord, J., Widom, C.S., and Crowell, N.A., eds. (2001). Juvenile Crime, Juvenile Justice. Panel on Juvenile Crime: Prevention, Treatment, and Control. Washington, DC: National Academy Press.

McKernan, Signe., Ratcliffe, C., and Vinopal, K. (2009). "Do Assets Help Families Cope with Adverse Events?" Washington, DC: The Urban Institute.

Meek, P. 7 Stages of Human Life Cycle.

Melhuish, E., Ereky-Stevens, K., Petrogiannis, K., Ariescu, A., Penderi, E., Rentzou, K., Tawell, A., Leseman, P., and Broekhuisen, M. (2014). A Review of Research On The Effects of Early Childhood Education And Care (ECEC) On Child Development.

Mental Health America, (2015). Position Statement 51: Children With Emotional Disorders In The Juvenile Justice System.

Mersky, J. P., and Topitzes, J. (2010). Comparing early adult outcomes of maltreated and non-maltreated children: A prospective longitudinal investigation Children and Youth Services Review, 32, 1086–1096

Mills, G B., and Amick, J. (2010). "Can Savings Help Overcome Income Instability?" Washington, DC: The Urban Institute.

Mitchum, P., and Moodie–Mills, A. C. (2014). Beyond Bullying: How Hostile School Climate Perpetuates the School-to-Prison Pipeline for LGBT Youth. Washington, D.C.: Center for American Progress

Moffitt, T. E., Arseneault, L., Jaffee, S. R., Kim-Cohen, J., Koenen, K. C., Odgers CL, et al. (2008). Research review: DSM-V conduct disorder: research needs for an evidence base. Journal of Child Psychology and Psychiatry. 2008; 49:3–33. [PubMed]

Moffitt, T. E., Caspi, A., Rutter, M., and Silva, P. (2001). Sex Differences in Antisocial Behaviour: Conduct Disorder, Delinquency, and Violence in the Dunedin Longitudinal Study (Cambridge University Press, 2001), p. 278.

Moffitt, T.E., Lynam, D., and Silva, P.A. (1994). Neuropsychological tests predict persistent male delinquency. Criminology 32:101-124.

Moore, K A., Vandivere, S., and Ehrle, J. (2000). "Turbulence and Child Well-Being." Assessing the New Federalism Brief B-16. Washington, DC: The Urban Institute.

Mustanski, B., Greene, G. J., Ryan, D., and Whitton, S. W. (2015). Feasibility, Acceptability, and Initial Efficacy of an Online Sexual Health Promotion Program for LGBT Youth: The Queer Sex Ed Intervention. J Sex Res 2015; 52(2): 220-30.

Nagin, D. S., & Paternoster, R. (1991). On the relationship of past to future participation in delinquency. Criminology, 29(2), 163-189.

National Conference of State Legislatures. Mental Health Needs of Juvenile Offenders.

National Mental Health Association (NMHA), (2004). In: Mental Health Treatment for Youth in The Juvenile Justice System: A Compendium of Promising Practices. John D., Catherine T., editors. MacArthur Foundation; Chicago, IL, USA: 2004

National Research Council. (1986). Criminal Careers and Career Criminals, A. Blumstein, J. Cohen, J.A. Roth, and C.A. Visher, eds. Washington, DC: National Academy Press.

National Scientific Council on the Developing Child. (2007). "Excessive Stress Disrupts the Architecture of the Developing Brain." Working Paper 3. Cambridge, MA: Center on the Developing Child, Harvard University.

Ney, B. (2015). 10 Facts About Women in Jails. Hope rises.

NICHD ECCRN. (1997a). Child care in the first year of life. Merrill-Palmer Quarterly, 43, 340-360.

NICHD Early Child Care Research Network. Are there long-term effects of early child care? Child Development 2007; 78(3):681–701.

NICHD Early Child Care Research Network. The effects of infant child care on infant-mother attachment security: Results of the NICHD study of early child care. Child Development 1997; 68 (5):860-879.

NICHD Early Child Care Research Network. Does the amount of time spent in child care predict socioemotional adjustment during the transition to kindergarten? Child Development 2003; 74 (4):976-1005.

NICHD Early Child Care Research Network. Child care and mother-child interaction in the first three years of life. Developmental Psychology 1999; 35 (6):1399-1413.

NKJV. Proverbs 22:6

Office of Child Development (OCD). Juvenile Justice: Rethinking Punitive Approaches To Addressing Juvenile Crime.

Office of Juvenile Justice and Delinquency Prevention (OJJDP). (1995). Bridging the child welfare and juvenile justice systems. Washington, DC, National Institute of Justice.

Office of the Surgeon General. (2001). Youth Violence: A Report of the Surgeon General. Washington, DC: U.S. Department of Health and Human Services, Office of the Secretary, Office of Public Health and Science, Office of the Surgeon General.

OJJDP Statistical Briefing Book. Online. Date=2010. Released on December 09, 2011.

OJJDP Statistical Briefing Book. Online. Date=2008. Released on May 06, 2011.

OJJDP Statistical Briefing Book. (2012).

Pajer, K. A. (1998). "What Happens to 'Bad' Girls? A Review of the Adult Outcomes of Antisocial Adolescent Girls," American Journal of Psychiatry 155, no. 7 (1998): 862–70.

ParentHelp123, Child Development: Children Age 2 to 4 Years. http://www.parenthelp123.org/child-development/2-4

Patterson, G.R. (1976). The aggressive child: Victim and architect of a coercive system. Pp. 267-316 in Behavior Modification and Families: Vol. 1. Theory and Research, E.J. Marsh, L.C. Handy, and L.A. Hamerlynck, eds. New York: Brunner/Mazel.

Patterson, G.R. 1982. Punishment for Aggression. Chapter 6 in Coercive Family Process. 1982. Vol. 3, p118. Castalia Publishing Company

Patterson, G. R., DeBaryshe, B. D., & Ramsey, E. (1989). A developmental perspective on antisocial behavior. American Psychology, February; 44(2), 329-35.

Patterson, G. R., Reid, J. B., & Dishion, T. J. (1992). Antisocial boys. Eugene, OR: Castalia.

Pfefferbaum, B. (1997). Posttraumatic stress disorder in children: a review of the past ten years. J Am Acad Child Adolesc Psychiatry. 1997;36 (11):1503– 1511

Pianta, R. C., Barnett, S. W., Burchinal, M., & Thornburg, K. R. 2009. The Effects of Preschool Education: What We Know, How Public Policy Is or Is Not Aligned With the Evidence Base, and What We Need to Know. Psychological Science in the Public Interest, 10(2), 49-88.

Piquero, A. R., and Chung, H. L. (2001). "On the Relationship between Gender, Early Onset, and the Seriousness of Offending," Journal of Criminal Justice 29, no. 3 (2001): 189–206

Piquero, A.R., Farrington, D.P., Nagin, D., and Moffitt, T. (2010). Trajectories of offending and their relation to life failure in late middle age: findings from the Cambridge Study in Delinquent Development. Journal of Research in Crime and Delinquency. 2010; 47: 151–73.

Piquero, A. R., Farrington, D.P., and Blumstein, A. (2007). Key Issues in Criminal Career Research: New Analyses of the Cambridge Study in Delinquent Development, Cambridge, U.K.: Cambridge University Press, 2007

Plomin, R., & Rutter, M. (1998). Child development, molecular genetics, and what to do with genes once they are found. Child Development, 69, 1221–1240.

Prison Policy Initiative, (2013). Mass Incarceration: "The Whole Pie." Data from "Sarah Hockenberry: Juveniles in Residential Placement, 2010 (Juvenile Offenders and Victims: National Report Series, Bulletin, June 2013)" (PDF). US Department of Justice. Retrieved 2014-10-13.

Puckett, J. A., Woodward, E. N., Mereish, E. H., and Pantalone, D. W. (2015). Parental Rejection Following Sexual Orientation Disclosure: Impact on Internalized Homophobia, Social Support, and Mental Health. LGBT Health 2015; 2(3): 265-9.

Pulkkinen, L., and Pitkanen, T. (1993). "Continuities in Aggressive Behavior from Childhood to Adulthood," Aggressive Behavior 19, no. 4 (1993): 249–63.

Pynoos, R. Traumatic stress and developmental psychopathology in children and adolescents. In: Oldham JM, Riba MB, Tasman A, eds. Review of Psychiatry. DC: American Psychiatric Association Press; 1993:205– 238Vol 12. Washington

Quackenbush, Thomm, Juvenile Justice: A Reference Handbook, 2nd Edition: A Reference Handbook

Raine, A., Brennan, P., and Mednick, S.A. (1994). Birth complications combined with early maternal rejection at age 1 year predispose to violent crime at age 18 years. Archives of General Psychiatry 53:544-549.

Raphael, S., & Winter-Ember, R. (2001). Identifying the effect of unemployment on crime. Journal of Law and Economics, 44, 259–283.

Reid, J. B. (1993). Prevention of conduct disorder before and after school entry: Relating interventions to developmental findings. Development & Psychopathology, 5, 243-262.

Reza, A., Krug, E.G., and Mercy, J.A. (2001). Epidemiology of violent deaths in the world. Injury Prevention, 2001, 7:104–111.

Roberts, R., Atkins, C., and Rosenblatt A. (1998). Prevalence of psychopathology among children and adolescents. Am. J. Psychiatry. 1998;155:715–725

Robins, L.N. (1978). Sturdy childhood predictors of adult antisocial behavior: Replications from longitudinal studies. Psychological Medicine 8:611-622.

Robbins, P. C., Monahan, J., and Silver, E. (2003). "Mental Disorder, Violence, and Gender," Law and Human Behavior 27, no. 6 (2003): 561–71.

Rossman, B.B.R. Longer term effects of children's exposure to domestic violence. In: Graham-Bermann SA, Edelson JL, eds. Domestic Violence in the Lives of Children: The Future of Research, Intervention, and Social Policy. Washington, DC: American Psychological Association; 2001:35–65

Rumbold, A R., Giles, L C., Whitrow, M J., Steele, E J., Davies, E C., Davies, J M., and Moore, V M. (2012). "The Effects of House Moves during Early Childhood on Child Mental Health at Age 9 Years." BMC Public Health 12(583).

Russell, S. T., Ryan, C., Toomey, R. B., Diaz, R. M., and Sanchez, J. (2011). Lesbian, gay, bisexual, and transgender adolescent school victimization: implications for young adult health and adjustment. Journal of School Health. 2011; 81(5):223-30.

Rutter, M., (1997). Nature-nurture integration: The example of antisocial behavior, American Psychologist, 52, 390-398.

Rutter, M., Dunn, J., Plomin, R., Simonoff, E., Pickles, A., Maughan, B., Ormel, J., Meyer, J., & Eaves, L. (1997). Integrating nature and nurture: Implications of person-environment correlations and interactions for developmental psychology, Development and Psychopathology, 9, 3335-364

Rutter, M., and Giller, H. (1983). Juvenile Delinquency: Trends and Perspectives. Harmondsworth, England: Penguin.

Rutter, M., Giller, H. & Hagell, A. (1998). Antisocial behavior by young people, New York: Cambridge University Press.

Rutter, M., & Plomin, R. (1997). Opportunities for psychiatry from genetic findings. British Journal of Psychiatry, 171, 209–219.

Ryan, C., Huebner, D., Diaz, R. M., and Sanchez, J. (2009). Family rejection as a predictor of negative health outcomes in white and Latino lesbian, gay, and bisexual young adults. Pediatrics 2009; 123: 346–352.

Ryan, C., Russell, S. T., Huebner, D., Diaz, R., and Sanchez, J. (2010). Family acceptance in adolescence and the health of LGBT young adults. J Child Adolesc Psychiatr Nurs 2010; 23(4): 205-13.

Ryan, J., Herz, D., Hernandez, P.M., & Marshall, J.M. (2007). Maltreatment and delinquency: Investigating child welfare bias in juvenile justice processing Children and Youth Services Review, 29(8), 1035–1050

Ryan, J., and Testa, M. (2005). Child maltreatment and juvenile delinquency: Investigating the role of placement and placement instability Children and Youth Services Review, 27, 227–249

Saewcy, E. M., Konishi, C., Rose, H. A., and Homma, Y. (2014). School-based strategies to reduce suicidal ideation, suicide attempts, and discrimination among sexual minority and heterosexual adolescents in Western Canada. International Journal of Child, Youth and Family Studies 2014; 1:89–112

Sampson, R.J., and Laub, J.H. (1993). Crime in the Making: Pathways and Turning Points Through Life. Cambridge, MA: Harvard University Press.

Sampson, R. J., Laub, J. H., and Wimer, C. (2006). "Does Marriage Reduce Crime? A Counter-Factual Approach to Within-Individual Causal Effects," Criminology 44, no. 3 (2006): 465–508

Sandstrom, H., and Huerta, S. (2013). The Negative Effects of Instability on Child Development: A Research Synthesis. Low-Income Working Families Discussion Paper 3. Copyright © September 2013. The Urban Institute.

Sarah, S. 2012. "The difference between discipline and child abuse". Demand Media. Retrieved 29 November 2012.

Scaccia, A. (2016). How to Identify and Treat Antisocial Behavior in Children.

Schneider, B., Atteberry, A., and Owens, A. (2005). Family matters: Family structure and child outcomes. 2005; 1-42. Birmingham, AL. Alabama Policy Institute.

Scottsdale, B. (2015). Long-Term Effects of Spoiling Children.

Sedlak, A. J., and McPherson, K. (2010). Conditions of Confinement: Findings from the Survey of Youth in Residential Placement. Washington, DC: U.S. Department of Justice, Office of Justice Programs, Office of Juvenile Justice and Delinquency Prevention

Seguin, J.R., Pihl, R.O., Harden, P.W., Tremblay, R.E., and Boulerice, B. (1995). Cognitive and neuropsychological characteristics of physically aggressive boys. Journal of Abnormal Psychology 104(4):614-624

Shelton, D. (2005). Patterns of treatment services and costs for young offenders with mental disorders. J. Child. Adolesc. Psych. Nurs. 2005;18:103–112. doi: 10.1111/j.1744-6171.2005.00013.x.

Shonkoff, J P. (2013). "Driving Science-Based Innovation to Reduce Intergenerational Poverty." Keynote address at the Welfare Research and Evaluation Conference, Washington, DC, May 29.

Shonkoff, J P., and Garner, A S. (2011). "The Lifelong Effects of Early Childhood Adversity and Toxic Stress." Pediatrics 129: 232–46.

Shover, N. (1996). Great pretenders: pursuits and careers of persistent thieves. Boulder, CO: Westview

Sickmund M. (2004) Juveniles in corrections. Juvenile offenders and victims national report series. Washington, DC: Office of Juvenile Justice and Delinquency Prevention.

Sickmund, M., Sladky, T.J., Kang, W., & Puzzanchera, C. (2011). "Easy Access to the Census of Juveniles in Residential Placement.

Siegel, D.J. (1999). The Developing Mind: Toward a Neurobiology of Intrapersonal Experience. New York, NY: Guilford Press; 1999

Siegel, Larry. J. (2007). Criminology, New York: McGraw Hill Inc. Ltd.

Silverthorn, P., and Frick, P. J. (1999). Developmental pathways to antisocial behavior: the delayed-onset pathway in girls. Dev Psychopathol. 1999 Winter; 11(1):101-26, PMID: 10208358.

Simmons, R., Whitbeck, L., Conger, R., and Conger, K. (1991). Parenting factors, social skills, and value commitments as precursors to school failure, involvement with deviant peers, and delinquent behavior. Journal of Youth and Adolescence 20:645-664.

Simons, R.L., Lin, K.H., Gordon, L., Brody, G.H., Murry, V.M., and Conger, R.D. (2002). Community differences in the association between parenting practices and child conduct problems. J Marriage Fam. 2002; 64: 331-345.

Simons, R.L., Wu, C., Conger, R.D., and Lorenz, F.O. (1994). Two routes to delinquency: Differences between early and late starters in the impact of parenting and deviant peers. Criminology 32:247-275.

Skinner, B. F. (1938). The behavior of organisms. New York: D. Appleton-Century Co., 1938.

Skowyra, K. R. & Cocozza, J.J., (2007). Blueprint for Change: A Comprehensive Model for the Identification and Treatment of Youth with Mental Health Needs in Contact with the Juvenile Justice System. Delmar, NY: National Center for Mental Health and Juvenile Justice (2007).

Smutt, M., and Miranda, J.L.E. (1998). El Salvador: socializacio´n y violencia juvenil. [El Salvador: socialization and juvenile violence.] In: Ramos CG, ed. America Central en los noventa: problemas de juventud. [Central America in the 90s: youth problems.] San Salvador, Latin American Faculty of Social Sciences, 1998:151–187.

Spekman, N. J. (1993). An exploration of risk and resilience in the lives of individuals with learning disabilities. Learning Disabilities Research and Practice, 8 (1), 11-18.

Stack, D. M., Serbin, L. A., Schwartzman, A. E., Ledingham, J. E and De Genna, N. (2005). Girls' Aggression across the Life Course: Long-Term Outcomes and Intergenerational Risk (Cambridge University Press, 2005).

Statistics Canada. Youth Court Statistics 2002–2003. Ottawa, ON: Canadian Centre for Justice Statistics; 2004.

Steinberg, L. (1987). Single parents, stepparents, and the susceptibility of adolescents to antisocial peer pressure. Child Development 58:269-275.

Stevens, A H., and Schaller, J. (2011). "Short-Run Effects of Parental Job Loss on Children's Academic Achievement." Economics of Education Review 30(2): 289–99.

Stewart, A., Livingston, M., and Denison, S. (2008). Transitions and turning points: Examining the links between child maltreatment and juvenile offending Child Abuse and Neglect, 32(1), 51–66

Stirling, J. (Jr)., and Amaya-Jackson, L. (2008). Understanding the Behavioral and Emotional Consequences of Child Abuse. Pediatrics, September 2008, VOLUME 122 / ISSUE 3

Stoddard-Dare, P., Mallett, C., and Boitel, C. (2011). Association between mental health disorders and juveniles' detention for a personal crime. Child. Adolesc. Ment. Health. 2011;16:208–213. doi: 10.1111/j.1475-3588.2011.00599.x.

Styron, T., and Janoff-Bulman, R. (1997). Childhood attachment and abuse: long-term effects on adult attachment, depression, and conflict resolution. Child Abuse Negl.1997; 21 (10):1015– 1023

Suh-Ruu, O., and Reynolds, A. J. (2010). Childhood Predictors of Young Adult Male Crime. Child Youth Serv Rev. 2010 Aug 1; 32(8): 1097–1107. doi: 10.1016/j.childyouth.2010.02.009.

Swain, B. The Effects of Poor Parental Care on a Child's Development. http://oureverydaylife.com/effects-poor-parental-care-childs-development-7745.html

Table C2. Household Relationship and Living Arrangements of Children under 18 Years, by Age and Sex: 2012," US Census Bureau, http://www.census.gov/hhes/families/data/cps2012.html, accessed July 29, 2012.

Takeda, Y. (2000). Aggression in relation to childhood depression: A study of Japanese 3rd-6th graders. Jpn. J. Dev. Psychol. 2000;11:1–11.

Tarling, R. (1993). Analyzing Offending: Data, Models, and Interpretations (London: Her Majesty's Stationery Office, 1993), p. 40.

Taylor, E. (1994). Syndromes of attention deficit and over-activity, in M. Rutter, E. Taylor & L. Hersov (Eds.), Child and adolescent psychiatry: Modern approaches, 3rd ed., 285-308, Oxford: Blackwell Scientific.

Taylor, E., Sandberg, S., Thorley, G. & Giles, S. (1991). The epidemiology of childhood hyperactivity, Oxford: Oxford University Press

Teacher, Law. (November 2013). Poor Parental Supervision Contribute Psychologically.

Tehrani, J., & Mednick, S. (2000). Genetic factors and criminal behavior. Federal Probation, 64, 24-28.

Teicher, M.H., Andersen, S.L., Polcari, A., Anderson, C.M., and Navalta, C.P. (2002). Developmental neurobiology of childhood stress and trauma. Psychiatr Clin North Am.2002; 25 (2):397– 426

Teicher, M.H., Dumont, N.L., Ito, Y., Vaituzis, C., Giedd, J.N., and Andersen, S.L. (2004). Childhood neglect is associated with reduced corpus callosum area. Biol Psychiatry.2004; 56 (2):80– 85

Teplin, L. A., Abram, K. M., McClelland, G. M., Dulcan, M. K., and Mericle, A. A. (2002). Psychiatric disorders in youth in juvenile detention. Arch. Gen. Psychiatry. 2002;59:1133–1143. doi: 10.1001/archpsyc.59.12.1133.

Thapar, A., Harold, G. & McGuffin, P., (1998). Life events and depressive symptoms in childhood – Shared genes or shared adversity? A research note. Journal of child psychology and psychiatry and allied disciplines, 39, 1153-1158.

The American Heritage Dictionary of the English Language, Fourth Edition. 2000. Houghton Mifflin Company.

The British Psychological Society. (2013). Antisocial Behavior and Conduct Disorders in Children and Young People: The Nice Guideline on Recognition, Intervention and Management. Commissioned by the National Institute for Health and Care Excellence. Printed in Great Britain by Stanley L. Hunt (Printers) Ltd, ISBN-: 978-1-908020-61-1.

The National Academies Press. (2001). Juvenile Crime, Juvenile Justice: The Development of Delinquency. The National Academies of Sciences Engineering Medicine.

The National Academies Press. (2015). Transforming the Workforce for Children Birth Through Age 8: A Unifying Foundation.

Thornberry, T.P., Krohn, M.D., Lizotte, A.J., and Chard-Wierschem, D. (1993). The role of juvenile gangs in facilitating delinquent behavior. Journal of Research in Crime and Delinquency 30(1):55-87.

Tremblay, R.E., and LeMarquand, D. (2001). Individual risk and protective factors. In Child Delinquents: Development, Intervention, and Service Needs, edited by R. Loeber and D.P. Farrington. Thousand Oaks, CA: Sage Publications, pp. 137–164.

Uggen, C. (2012). Crime and the great recession. Stanford, CA: Stanford Center on Poverty and Inequality, Recession Trends Series

Uggen, C. (1999). Ex-offenders and the conformist alternative: A Job quality model of work and crime. Social Problems, 46 (1), 127–151.

Uggen, C., Manza, J., and Behrens, A. (2004). Less than the average citizen: stigma, role transition, and the civic reintegration of convicted felons. In S. Maruna & R. Immarigeon (Eds.), After crime and punishment: pathways to offender reintegration (pp. 258–290). Cullompton, Devon: Willan Publishing

Uggen, C., and Wakefield, S. (2007). What have we learned from longitudinal studies of adolescent employment and crime? In A. Liberman (Ed.), The long view of crime: a synthesis of longitudinal research (pp. 189–218). New York: Springer.

Ulzen, T. P. M., and Hamilton, H. (1998). The nature and characteristics of psychiatric comorbidity in incarcerated adolescents. Canadian Journal of Psychiatry. 1998; 43:57–63

Underwood, L. A., Washington, A. (2016). Mental Illness and Juvenile Offenders. Int J Environ Res Public Health. 2016 Feb; 13(2): 228. PMCID: PMC4772248 doi: 10.3390/ijerph13020228

United States Department of Justice (USDJ), (2011). Department of Justice Activities under the Civil. Rights Institutionalized Persons Act: Fiscal Year 2010. CRIPA; Washington, DC, USA: 2011

US Census Bureau. (2006). Accessed on May 1, 2008.

US Census Bureau, "Census Bureau Reports National Mover Rate Increases after a Record Low in 2011," newsroom release CB12-240, December 12, 2012.

Utting, D. 2007. Parenting and the different ways it can affect children's lives: research evidence. Published by the Joseph Rowntree Foundation, The Homestead, 40 Water End, York YO30 6WP.

Van Voorhis, P., and Presser, L. (2001). Classification of women offenders: A national assessment of current practice. Washington, DC: U.S. Department of Justice, National Institute of Corrections.

Wakschlag, L. S., and Hans, S. L. (1999). "Relation of Maternal Responsiveness during Infancy to the Development of Behavior Problems in High-Risk Youths," Developmental Psychology 35, no. 2 (1999): 569–79.

Wald, J., and Losen, D. (2003). Defining and redirecting a school-to-prison pipeline. New Dir. Youth Dev. 2003;2003:9–15. doi: 10.1002/yd.51.

Walker, H. M., Colvin, G., & Ramsey, E. (1995). Antisocial behavior in school: Strategies and best practices. Pacific Grove, CA: Brooks/Cole

Walker, H. M., Horner, R. H., Sugai, G., Bullis, J. R., Bricker, D., & Kaufman, M. (1996). Integrated approaches to preventing antisocial behavior patterns among school-age children and youth. Journal of Emotional and Behavioral Disorders, 4 (4), 194-209.

Warren, J. (2012). A New Way to Fight Juvenile Crime in Chicago, The Daily Beast December 7/13/2012.

Wasserman, G. A., McReynolds, L. S., Lucas, C. P., Fisher, P., and Santos L. (2002). The voice DISC-IV with incarcerated male youths: Prevalence of disorder. J. Am. Acad. Child. Adolesc. Psychiatry. 2002;41:314–321. doi: 10.1097/00004583-200203000-00011

Wasserman, G.A., and Seracini, A.G. (2001). Family risk factors and interventions. In Child Delinquents: Development, Intervention, and Service Needs, edited by R. Loeber and D.P. Farrington. Thousand Oaks, CA: Sage Publications, pp. 165–189.

Wells, L.E., and Rankin, J.H. (1991). Families and delinquency: A meta-analysis of the impact of broken homes. Social Problems 38:71-93.

West, D.J., and Farrington, D.P. (1973). Who Becomes Delinquent? London, England: Heinemann.

Widom, C.S. (1989). Child abuse, neglect, and violent criminal behavior. Criminology, 244:160–166.

Widom, C.S. (1989). The cycle of violence. Science 244:160-166

Widom, C. (1996). Childhood sexual abuse and its criminal consequences Society, 33, 47–53

Widom, C., and Maxfield, M. (2001). An update on the "cycle of violence." Research in Brief Washington, DC: National Institute of Justice, US Department of Justice, Office of Justice Programs

wikiHow to Discipline a Child. http://www.wikihow.com/Discipline-a-Child

Wikipedia. Juvenile Justice and Delinquency Prevention Act. Retrieved from: https://en.wikipedia.org/wiki/Juvenile_Justice_and_Delinquency_Prevention_Act

Wikstrom POH. (1985). Everyday violence in contemporary Sweden. Stockholm, National Council for Crime Prevention.

Williamson, M.S. Information on Incarcerated Women & Girls. Retrieved from: https://theoperationrestoration.com/information-on-incarcerated-women-girls/

Wilson, J.Q., and Herrnstein, R.J. (1985). Crime and Human Nature. New York: Simon & Schuster.

Wodarski, J.S., Kurtz, P.D., Gaudin, J.M, (Jr)., and Howling, P.T. (1990). Maltreatment and the school-aged child: major academic, socioemotional, and adaptive outcomes. Social Work.1990; 35 (6):506– 513

Wolin, S. J., & Wolin, S. (1994). The resilient self: How survivors of troubled families rise above adversity. New York: Villard Books.

Yeung, W J., and Hofferth, S. (1998). "Family Adaptations to Income and Job Loss in the U.S." Journal of Family and Economic Issues 19(3): 255–83.

Yochelson, S., and Samenow, S.E. (1990). The Criminal Personality, Volume I: A Profile for Change, New York: Jason Aronson, 1976; and Walters, G., The Criminal Lifestyle: Patterns of Serious Criminal Conduct, Newbury Park, Calif.: Sage Publications, 1990.

Youth violence, (2001). A report of the Surgeon General. Washington, DC, United States Department of Health and Human Services.

Youth Violence: World Report on Violence and Health.

Youth.gov. Prevention & Early Intervention.

Zaroban, A. L. (2006). Defining, Identifying and Addressing Antisocial Behavior in Children Ages 4-7: The Perspectives of Selected Elementary Principals in a Midwestern City School District. University of Nebraska- Lincoln. DigitalCommons@University of Nebraska - Lincoln.

Zeira, Y., and Baldwin, M. (2016). Pioneers in Young Adult Justice: 10 Initiatives and Programs Improving Criminal Justice for Young Adults.

Zimmer, M.H., and Panko, L.M. (2006). Developmental status and service use among children in the child welfare system: a national survey. Arch Pediatric Adolescent Med.2006; 160 (2):183– 188

Zingraff, M.T., Leiter, J., Myers, K.A., & Johnsen, M.C. (1993). Child maltreatment and youthful problem behavior Criminology, 31(2), 173–202

Zoccolillo, M., Paquette, D., and Tremblay, R. (2005). "Maternal Conduct Disorder and the Risk for the Next Generation," in The Development and Treatment of Girlhood Aggression, edited by Debra Pepler and others (Mahwah, N.J.: Lawrence Erlbaum Associates Publishers, 2005), pp. 225–52.

Biography

Elvis Slaughter, M.S.C.J. is an educator, consultant, publisher, author, retired sheriff's superintendent, fire and police commissioner, and criminologist. He has written and published books and articles since 2005, which include *Safer Jail and Prison Matters*.

Elvis also volunteers his time to community work and public speaking. Elvis is devoted to mentoring the next generation of leaders, and he loves exploring Chicago's vibrant jazz scene during his free time. He is a member of the American Correctional Association, American Jail Association, Illinois Sheriff's Association, Hammond Police Citizen Advisory Commission, and a member and past president of the Illinois Academy of Criminology.

Also by Elvis Slaughter, M.S.C.J.

The American Genocide
The Ghosts of Hollandale
Uncle Percy's Blessings
The Malcolm X Project
Epiphany Or Sin
Safer Jail and Prison Matters
Egomaniac

Available at Amazon.com and **www.elvisslaughter.com**